# THEOLOGY OF LOVE

## LOVE

Dr. Maxwell Shimba

Shimba Publishing, LLC.

Printed in the United States of America

# TABLE OF CONTENTS

Theology of Love
**Bibliography**

## PREFACE

Love is one of the most profound and multifaceted concepts known to humanity, touching every aspect of our existence. It is a force that transcends time and space, uniting people across cultures, languages, and generations. The theology of love seeks to explore this powerful force from a divine perspective, examining its origins, manifestations, and ultimate fulfillment in the relationship between God and humanity.

In this book, we embark on a journey to understand love through the lens of theology. We begin by exploring the nature of love as an attribute of God, delving into the depths of divine love that is expressed within the Trinity and extended to all of creation. By examining the biblical foundations of love, both in the Old and New Testaments, we seek to uncover the rich tapestry of love that is woven throughout the scriptures.

Our exploration is not limited to theoretical reflections; we also consider the practical applications of love in our daily lives. From family dynamics and church communities to broader societal interactions, we examine how the theology of love can transform relationships and foster a more compassionate and just world.

We acknowledge that the journey to understanding and living out divine love is fraught with challenges. Human frailties such as selfishness, pride, and the pain of suffering can impede our ability to fully embrace and express love. However, through the lens of forgiveness, reconciliation, and perseverance, we find hope and strength to overcome these obstacles.

Ultimately, this book aims to provide a holistic view of love that integrates theological insights with practical wisdom. We invite readers to engage deeply with the scriptures, reflect on their personal experiences, and apply the principles of divine love in their everyday lives.

May this exploration of the theology of love inspire and challenge you to grow in your understanding and practice of love, drawing you closer to the heart of God and to those around you. As we journey together, let us be reminded that love is not merely an abstract concept but a living, dynamic force that has the power to transform lives and bring us into deeper communion with our Creator.

Acknowledgments

This work would not have been possible without the support and encouragement of many individuals. I would like to express my deepest gratitude to my family, friends, and colleagues who have walked with me on this journey. Their love, wisdom, and prayers have been a constant source of strength.

I am also indebted to the countless theologians, scholars, and spiritual leaders whose writings and teachings have informed and enriched this study. Their dedication to exploring the depths of divine love has been both a guide and an inspiration.

Finally, I am grateful to the readers of this book. Your willingness to engage with these ideas and to seek a deeper understanding of love is a testament to the enduring power and relevance of this divine attribute. May you be blessed as you embark on this journey of discovery and transformation.

With heartfelt gratitude,

Dr. Maxwell Shimba

DR. MAXWELL SHIMBA

# CHAPTER 01

---

## THE DIVINE NATURE OF LOVE

1.1. Love as an Attribute of God

Understanding God as Love (1 John 4:8)

In the Bible, we find one of the most profound and succinct definitions of God's nature: "God is love" (1 John 4:8). This simple yet profound statement encapsulates the essence of who God is and serves as the foundation for our exploration of the theology of love. To truly understand love, we must first understand God, for He is the source and embodiment of all love.

The declaration that "God is love" does not merely suggest that God loves or that love is one of His many attributes. Rather, it implies that love is central to His very being. Love is not an ancillary characteristic of God but is fundamental to His nature. Every action of God, every command, and every interaction with humanity is rooted in His loving nature.

This concept challenges many traditional views of God that might emphasize His power, justice, or wrath without fully integrating these attributes with His love. While God is indeed powerful, just, and righteous, these qualities are always expressed in harmony with His love. To isolate any attribute from His loving nature is to misunderstand the very essence of God.

The Bible provides numerous passages that illustrate God's loving nature. From the Old Testament to the New Testament, we see a consistent revelation of God's love for His creation.

Creation as an Act of Love

The act of creation itself is a testament to God's love. In Genesis 1, we see a God who creates a world that is "good" and ultimately "very good." Humanity is created in His image, signifying a special relationship between God and His creation. This act of creation is not out of necessity but an overflow of divine love. God desired to share His love, and thus He created beings capable of experiencing and reciprocating that love.

Covenantal Love

Throughout the Old Testament, God's love is often depicted through His covenantal relationships with His people. The Hebrew word "hesed," often translated as "steadfast love," captures the enduring and faithful nature of God's love. In His covenant with Abraham, God promises to bless Abraham and his descendants, demonstrating a commitment that is rooted in love (Genesis 12:1-3).

The Exodus narrative further exemplifies God's love. Despite Israel's repeated failures and disobedience, God remains faithful to His covenant. He delivers them from slavery in Egypt, provides for them in the wilderness, and leads them to the Promised Land. These acts of salvation and provision are driven by His steadfast love.

Prophetic Expressions of Love

The prophets often speak of God's love, calling Israel to return to Him. Hosea, for example, portrays God's love for Israel through the metaphor of a husband and wife. Despite Israel's unfaithfulness, God's love remains unwavering. In Hosea 11:1-4, God is depicted as a loving parent who tenderly cares for His child, Israel, despite their rebellion.

Love in the Life and Ministry of Jesus

The fullest revelation of God's love is found in the person of Jesus Christ. In the New Testament, we see that Jesus' life and ministry are the ultimate expressions of divine love. The incarnation—God becoming flesh and dwelling among us (John 1:14)—is the supreme act of love. Jesus' teachings, miracles, and compassion for the marginalized all reflect the heart of a loving God.

The culmination of God's love is seen in the sacrificial death of Jesus on the cross. John 3:16 encapsulates this truth: "For God so loved the world that He gave His one and only Son, that whoever believes in Him shall not perish but have eternal life." The cross is the ultimate demonstration of God's love, where justice and mercy meet. Through Jesus' sacrifice, humanity is offered reconciliation with God, a profound act of love that restores the broken relationship caused by sin.

The Implications of God's Love

Understanding that "God is love" has profound implications for our theology, worship, and daily living. It shapes our understanding of God's actions and commands and influences how we relate to Him and others.

Every action of God is motivated by love. Whether it is His acts of creation, redemption, or sanctification, love is the driving force behind them all. This understanding provides a lens through which we can interpret God's actions in history and in our lives. Even when we encounter difficult circumstances or divine discipline, we can trust that God's love is at work for our ultimate good (Hebrews 12:6).

As recipients of God's love, we are called to respond in love. The Great Commandment, as articulated by Jesus, is to love God with all our heart, soul, mind, and strength, and to love our neighbor as ourselves (Mark 12:30-31). Our love for God is a response to His prior love for us (1 John 4:19). This love is not merely emotional but is expressed through obedience, worship, and service.

The love we receive from God is not meant to be hoarded but shared. Jesus calls His followers to love one another as He has loved them (John 13:34-35). This selfless, sacrificial love becomes a defining mark of the Christian community. By loving others, we reflect God's love for the world and become instruments of His grace and mercy.

Love as the Fulfillment of the Law

Paul, in his epistles, emphasizes that love is the fulfillment of the law (Romans 13:8-10). All commandments are summed up in the call to love. This underscores the idea that true obedience to God is rooted in love. Legalistic adherence to rules without love misses the heart of God's commands. Love guides our actions, ensuring that they align with God's will and character.

The statement "God is love" encapsulates the essence of God's nature and provides a foundation for understanding the theology of love. It calls us to a deeper relationship with God, marked by love and trust. It challenges us to reflect

God's love in our interactions with others, making love the central theme of our faith and practice.

As we continue our exploration of the theology of love, let us keep this foundational truth at the forefront: God's love is the source, sustainer, and goal of all things. May we be continually transformed by this love, growing in our capacity to love God and others with the same steadfast, sacrificial love that He has shown us.

## 1.1.0 THE IMPLICATIONS OF GOD'S LOVING NATURE FOR HIS CREATION

Understanding that "God is love" (1 John 4:8) brings with it a multitude of profound implications for His creation. When we comprehend that love is intrinsic to God's very being, it reshapes our understanding of the world and our place within it. In this chapter, we will explore how God's loving nature impacts creation, human relationships, and our ultimate purpose.

The act of creation is the first and most fundamental expression of God's love. In Genesis 1, we read that God created the heavens and the earth, culminating in the creation of humanity, which He declared "very good" (Genesis 1:31). This act was not born out of necessity or loneliness but out of an overflow of divine love. God, who exists in a perfect loving relationship within the Trinity, chose to create beings who could experience and reciprocate that love.

Being made in the image of God (Genesis 1:27) signifies that we are designed to reflect His loving nature. This imago Dei is foundational to our identity and purpose. As image-bearers, we are called to mirror God's love in our relationships, stewardship of creation, and in our worship. The intrinsic worth and dignity of every human being are rooted in this divine image, underscoring the universal call to love and respect one another.

The Sustaining Love of God

God's love is not a one-time act but a continuous provision and care for His creation. In Acts 17:28, Paul reminds us that "in Him, we live and move and have our being." God's sustaining love ensures that creation is upheld and that all living things are provided for. This is evident in Jesus' teaching in Matthew 6:26-30, where He points to God's care for the birds of the air and the lilies of the field, encouraging us to trust in His provision.

God's love is also redemptive. When humanity fell into sin, God's response was not one of abandonment but of a loving pursuit. The plan of redemption, culminating in the life, death, and resurrection of Jesus Christ, is the ultimate demonstration of God's sacrificial love. John 3:16

encapsulates this truth: "For God so loved the world that He gave His one and only Son, that whoever believes in Him shall not perish but have eternal life."

Through Christ's sacrifice, the broken relationship between God and humanity is restored. This redemptive love offers forgiveness, reconciliation, and the promise of eternal life. It calls us to repentance and invites us into a loving relationship with our Creator.

Love in Human Relationships

Understanding God's loving nature shapes how we relate to one another. Jesus summarized the Law and the Prophets with the command to love God and love our neighbor (Matthew 22:37-40). This dual commandment reflects the inseparable link between divine and human love. Our love for God is expressed through our love for others, and vice versa.

Christian love, or agape, is characterized by selflessness, sacrifice, and unconditional commitment. It is a love that mirrors God's own love for us. In 1 Corinthians 13, Paul provides a beautiful description of agape love, highlighting its qualities of patience, kindness, humility, and perseverance. This love is not dependent on the worthiness of the recipient but is a reflection of the giver's nature.

Family and Community

The implications of God's love extend to our family and community relationships. In Ephesians 5:25, husbands are called to love their wives as Christ loved the church, demonstrating a sacrificial and nurturing love. Similarly, the Christian community is called to embody love, unity, and mutual care (Acts 2:42-47). The early church's example of sharing and supporting one another reflects the outworking of God's love in a communal setting.

The Call to Stewardship

As stewards of God's creation, we are called to reflect His loving care for the environment. This stewardship is rooted in the understanding that the earth and all its resources are gifts of God's love, entrusted to us for responsible use and care. In Genesis 2:15, Adam is placed in the Garden of Eden to "work it and take care of it," signifying the human responsibility to nurture and protect the natural world.

Ethical Living

Living out God's love also entails ethical behavior in all aspects of life. This includes honesty, integrity, justice, and compassion. The prophetic literature of the Old Testament frequently calls God's people to live out His love through acts of justice and mercy (Micah 6:8). Jesus' parable of the Good Samaritan (Luke 10:25-37) underscores the importance of extending love and compassion beyond cultural and social boundaries.

The Hope of Eternal Love

Eschatological Fulfillment

The ultimate fulfillment of God's love will be realized in the eschaton—the final consummation of all things. Revelation 21:3-4 paints a picture of a new heaven and a new earth where God dwells with His people, wiping away every tear and abolishing death, mourning, crying, and pain. This eternal communion with God is the culmination of His redemptive love, where we will experience perfect and unending love.

Understanding the future hope of God's love impacts how we live in the present. It gives us a perspective that transcends temporal struggles and suffering. Paul speaks of this hope in Romans 8:38-39, assuring us that nothing can separate us from the love of God in Christ Jesus. This assurance empowers us to live boldly and love deeply, knowing that our ultimate destiny is secure in God's loving hands.

The implications of God's loving nature for His creation are vast and transformative. From the very act of creation to the sustaining and redemptive work of God, love is the thread that weaves through the entire narrative of

Scripture. As recipients of this divine love, we are called to reflect it in our relationships, stewardship, and ethical living. Our hope is anchored in the eternal love of God, promising a future where His love will be perfectly realized.

As we continue to explore the theology of love, let us be mindful of the profound impact that understanding God's loving nature can have on our lives. May we be inspired to live out this love in all we do, drawing others to the heart of the God who is love.

## 1.2.0 LOVE IN THE TRINITY

Understanding the relational dynamics of love within the Trinity provides profound insights into the nature of God and His interaction with creation. The doctrine of the Trinity—one God in three persons: Father, Son, and Holy Spirit—reveals a divine community characterized by perfect love. This chapter delves into the theological foundations and implications of Trinitarian love, offering a deeper appreciation of how this divine relationship shapes our understanding of love.

The Trinity: A Community of Love

The concept of the Trinity, while complex and mysterious, is central to Christian theology. Scripture provides glimpses into this divine relationship. In Matthew 28:19, Jesus commands His disciples to baptize "in the name of the Father and of the Son and of the Holy Spirit," indicating the distinct persons within the Godhead. Additionally, passages like John 1:1-2 and 14:16-17 highlight the distinct yet unified nature of the Father, Son, and Holy Spirit.

Perichoresis: The Divine Dance

The term "perichoresis" describes the interpenetrating and co-inherent relationship among the Trinity's persons. Often referred to as the "divine dance," perichoresis suggests a dynamic, intimate relationship characterized by mutual indwelling and love. Each person of the Trinity exists in perfect harmony and unity, constantly giving and receiving love. This eternal exchange of love is foundational to God's nature and is reflected in His interactions with creation.

The Father's Love for the Son and Spirit

Throughout the Gospels, we see the Father's love for the Son explicitly expressed. At Jesus' baptism, a voice from heaven declares, "This is my Son, whom I love; with him, I am well pleased" (Matthew 3:17). This affirmation is repeated at the Transfiguration (Matthew 17:5). The Father's love is one of delight, pleasure, and unwavering affirmation, demonstrating a deep relational bond.

The Father's love is also demonstrated through His sending of the Son and the Spirit. In John 3:16, we learn that

God so loved the world that He gave His only Son. This act of sending is not out of compulsion but out of love for humanity and for the Son. Similarly, Jesus promises the coming of the Holy Spirit, sent by the Father, to guide and comfort believers (John 14:26). The sending of the Son and Spirit reflects the Father's desire to share His love with creation.

### The Son's Love for the Father and Spirit

### Obedience and Honor

Jesus' earthly ministry is marked by His love for and obedience to the Father. In John 14:31, Jesus states, "I love the Father and do exactly what my Father has commanded me." This obedience is not merely dutiful but is rooted in a deep, loving relationship. Jesus honors the Father, seeking to glorify Him in all He does (John 17:4).

Jesus' love for the Spirit is evident in His promise to send the Advocate to His followers. In John 16:7, Jesus explains that it is for the disciples' good that He goes away, for then the Holy Spirit will come. This promise reflects Jesus' understanding of the Spirit's essential role in the lives of believers and His desire to ensure they are not left alone. The mutual respect and recognition between the Son and Spirit further illustrate the Trinitarian love dynamic.

The Spirit's Love for the Father and Son

Empowering and Glorifying

The Holy Spirit's role in the Trinity includes empowering and glorifying both the Father and the Son. In John 16:13-14, Jesus describes how the Spirit will guide believers into all truth and glorify Him by taking what is His and making it known to them. The Spirit's work is intrinsically connected to the Father and the Son, reflecting their will and bringing glory to them.

The Spirit's love is also manifested in His indwelling presence within believers. Romans 5:5 states that "God's love has been poured out into our hearts through the Holy Spirit, who has been given to us." The Spirit's indwelling enables believers to experience and participate in the Trinitarian love, transforming their lives and empowering them to love others.

Implications of Trinitarian Love for Believers

The love within the Trinity serves as the ultimate model for human relationships. Just as the Father, Son, and Spirit exist in perfect unity and self-giving love, believers are called to emulate this relational dynamic. In John 13:34-35, Jesus commands His disciples to love one another as He has loved them, thus reflecting Trinitarian love in their community.

The Trinity exemplifies unity in diversity. Each person of the Trinity is distinct yet united in essence and purpose. This unity in diversity provides a powerful model for the church, encouraging believers to celebrate their diverse gifts and roles while striving for unity in love and purpose (1 Corinthians 12:12-14).

Believers are invited to participate in the love of the Trinity. Through the indwelling of the Holy Spirit, we are drawn into the relational life of the Triune God. This participation transforms our understanding of love from a mere human emotion to a divine calling. As we grow in our relationship with God, we become conduits of His love to the world.

The Spirit's presence empowers believers to love as God loves. Galatians 5:22-23 lists the fruit of the Spirit, with love being the first mentioned. This divine empowerment enables believers to exhibit the selfless, sacrificial love that characterizes the Trinity. In our human relationships, this love manifests in forgiveness, service, and a commitment to the well-being of others.

The relational dynamics of love within the Trinity offer a profound and transformative understanding of God's nature. The perfect, self-giving love shared between the Father, Son, and Holy Spirit serves as both a model and a source of empowerment for believers. As we reflect on the Trinitarian love, we are invited to deepen our relationship with God and embody His love in our interactions with others.

The love within the Trinity is not static but dynamic, characterized by an eternal exchange of giving and receiving. This divine dance of love calls us to a higher standard of love in our own lives, one that mirrors the unity, diversity, and selflessness of the Triune God. As we continue to explore the theology of love, let us be inspired by the perfect love of the Trinity and strive to reflect it in all we do.

## 1.2.1 THE FATHER, SON, AND HOLY SPIRIT AS THE PERFECT MODEL OF LOVE

The Trinity—Father, Son, and Holy Spirit—serves as the perfect model of love, providing profound insights into the nature of God and His interaction with creation. The relationships within the Trinity exemplify perfect love, unity, and diversity, offering a divine blueprint for understanding and practicing love in our own lives. This chapter explores how the Father, Son, and Holy Spirit model perfect love and the implications of this divine example for human relationships and community.

The Father's Affirmation and Delight in the Son

Throughout the Gospels, the Father's love for the Son is vividly depicted. At Jesus' baptism, the heavens open, and a voice declares, "This is my Son, whom I love; with him, I am well pleased" (Matthew 3:17). This declaration is repeated at the Transfiguration (Matthew 17:5). These moments underscore the Father's delight and affirmation of the Son, revealing a deep relational bond rooted in love.

The Father's love is also evident in His sending of the Son into the world. John 3:16 states, "For God so loved the world that He gave His one and only Son, that whoever believes in Him shall not perish but have eternal life." This act of sending His beloved Son demonstrates the Father's sacrificial love, willingness to give what is most precious for the sake of humanity.

The Father's Relationship with the Holy Spirit

The Father's love for the Holy Spirit is reflected in the Spirit's role within the Trinity. The Spirit proceeds from the Father, as described in John 15:26: "When the Advocate comes, whom I will send to you from the Father—the Spirit of truth who goes out from the Father—He will testify about me." This procession signifies a relationship of love and mutual indwelling, where the Spirit actively participates in the Father's mission and work.

The Son's Love for the Father and the Spirit

Obedience and Honor to the Father

Jesus' earthly ministry is marked by His love for and obedience to the Father. In John 14:31, Jesus declares, "I love the Father and do exactly what my Father has commanded me." This obedience is not merely dutiful but arises from a deep, loving relationship. Jesus' desire to honor and glorify the Father is evident throughout His ministry (John 17:4).

Jesus' prayer in John 17 further highlights this love, as He prays for the unity of believers, reflecting the unity He shares with the Father: "That all of them may be one, Father, just as you are in me and I am in you" (John 17:21). This unity is rooted in divine love, exemplifying perfect relational harmony.

Promising and Sending the Holy Spirit

Jesus' love for the Holy Spirit is demonstrated in His promise to send the Spirit to His followers. In John 16:7, Jesus tells His disciples, "But very truly I tell you, it is for your good that I am going away. Unless I go away, the Advocate will not come to you; but if I go, I will send Him to you." This promise reflects Jesus' understanding of the Spirit's essential role and His desire to ensure believers are not left alone.

Jesus' description of the Spirit as the "Advocate" who will guide, teach, and comfort His followers (John 14:26) reveals His deep respect and love for the Spirit's work. This relationship within the Trinity is characterized by mutual recognition and honor, each person upholding and glorifying the other.

The Holy Spirit's Love for the Father and the Son
Empowering and Glorifying

The Holy Spirit's role within the Trinity includes empowering and glorifying both the Father and the Son. In John 16:13-14, Jesus describes how the Spirit will guide believers into all truth and glorify Him by taking what is His and making it known to them. The Spirit's work is intrinsically connected to the mission of the Father and the Son, reflecting their will and bringing glory to them.

Indwelling Believers

The Spirit's love is also manifested in His indwelling presence within believers. Romans 5:5 states, "God's love has been poured out into our hearts through the Holy Spirit, who has been given to us." The Spirit's indwelling enables believers to experience and participate in the Trinitarian love, transforming their lives and empowering them to love others.

The Holy Spirit's role in the life of the believer is one of continual presence and guidance. The Spirit teaches, comforts, convicts, and sanctifies, all expressions of divine love aimed at drawing believers into a deeper relationship with God and conforming them to the image of Christ.

The Trinity as a Model for Human Relationships

The Trinity exemplifies unity in diversity. Each person of the Trinity is distinct yet united in essence and purpose. This unity in diversity provides a powerful model for human relationships and community. Just as the Father, Son, and Holy Spirit exist in perfect relational harmony, believers are called to emulate this dynamic in their interactions with one another.

In the church, this model of unity and diversity is especially significant. Paul's metaphor of the body of Christ in 1 Corinthians 12 highlights how diverse gifts and roles come together to form a unified whole. Each member, though different, is essential and contributes to the health and function of the body, reflecting the Trinitarian model of love.

Self-Giving and Sacrificial Love

The love within the Trinity is characterized by self-giving and sacrifice. The Father gives the Son, the Son lays down His life, and the Spirit empowers and guides believers. This self-giving love serves as the ultimate example for how we are to love others. In Philippians 2:5-8, Paul urges believers to have the same mindset as Christ Jesus, who "made himself nothing by taking the very nature of a servant" and humbled Himself to the point of death on a cross.

This call to self-giving and sacrificial love challenges us to move beyond self-interest and embrace a love that seeks the good of others, even at a personal cost. It is a love that reflects the heart of the Triune God and transforms relationships and communities.

Mutual Honor and Respect

The relationships within the Trinity are marked by mutual honor and respect. Each person of the Trinity honors and glorifies the others, creating a dynamic of equality and mutuality. This model of mutual honor challenges hierarchical and authoritarian structures, promoting a relational dynamic based on respect and recognition of each person's value and contribution.

In practical terms, this means valuing and honoring the contributions and perspectives of others and fostering an environment where all can flourish. It calls for a culture of encouragement and affirmation, reflecting the divine love seen within the Trinity.

Implications for the Church and Society

Building a Loving Community

The church, as the body of Christ, is called to reflect the love and unity of the Trinity. This involves creating a community where love is the guiding principle, unity is pursued amidst diversity, and each member is valued and honored. The early church provides a model of such a community, as described in Acts 2:42-47, where believers shared life together, met each other's needs, and lived in harmony.

Witness to the World

The love modeled by the Trinity serves as a powerful witness to the world. In John 13:35, Jesus states, "By this everyone will know that you are my disciples if you love one another." The love within the Christian community, reflective of the divine love of the Trinity, becomes a testimony to the reality of God's love. It attracts others to the faith and demonstrates the transformative power of God's love in action.

Promoting Justice and Reconciliation

The Trinitarian model of love also has profound implications for social justice and reconciliation. Just as the Trinity embodies mutual respect, equality, and self-giving love, believers are called to work for justice and reconciliation in society. This involves addressing systems of inequality, advocating for the marginalized, and fostering relationships of mutual respect and dignity.

The Father, Son, and Holy Spirit as the perfect model of love offer a profound and transformative vision for understanding and practicing love. The relational dynamics within the Trinity—marked by unity, diversity, self-giving, and mutual honor—provide a divine blueprint for human relationships and community.

As we reflect on the perfect love of the Trinity, we are invited to deepen our relationship with God and embody His love in our interactions with others. This Trinitarian model of love calls us to a higher standard of love, one that transcends self-interest and embraces a self-giving, sacrificial love that transforms lives and communities.

May we strive to reflect the perfect love of the Trinity in all we do, drawing others to the heart of the God who is love. As we continue our exploration of the theology of love, let us be inspired by the divine example set by the Father, Son, and Holy Spirit, and seek to embody this perfect love in our daily lives.

## 1.2.2 CREATION AND LOVE

The concept of God's love as the foundation of creation is a profound and transformative idea. Understanding creation through the lens of divine love provides a rich perspective on the nature of the world, humanity's place within it, and our relationship with God and one another. This chapter explores how God's love is the cornerstone of creation and the implications of this foundational truth.

### The Act of Creation as an Expression of Divine Love

### The Genesis Account

The Bible begins with the majestic account of creation in Genesis 1. This narrative reveals a God who creates out of love, bringing order and beauty from chaos. Each act of creation, from the separation of light and darkness to the creation of living beings, is a testament to God's intentional and loving design. The repeated affirmation that creation is "good" (Genesis 1:4, 10, 12, 18, 21, 25) culminates in the creation of humanity, which God declares "very good" (Genesis 1:31).

### Humanity Made in God's Image

Human beings hold a unique place in creation, being made in the image of God (Genesis 1:27). This imago Dei signifies that humans are reflections of God's character, endowed with attributes that enable them to relate to God and each other. The capacity to love, reason, create, and steward the earth is rooted in this divine image. Being created in God's image is a profound expression of His love, granting humans intrinsic worth and dignity.

### Creation Reflects God's Loving Nature

### The Beauty and Order of Creation

The natural world, in all its complexity and beauty, reflects God's loving nature. Psalm 19:1 declares, "The heavens declare the glory of God; the skies proclaim the work of His hands." The intricate design and harmonious order of creation speak of a Creator who cares deeply about His work. Every element, from the smallest microorganism to the vast galaxies, displays a purposeful and loving design.

God's love is also evident in His provision and sustenance of creation. In Psalm 104, the psalmist marvels at how God provides for all creatures, ensuring they have food, water, and shelter. This divine care extends to the natural cycles and ecosystems that sustain life on earth. Jesus highlights this aspect of God's love in Matthew 6:26-30, encouraging His followers to trust in God's provision, as He cares even for the birds of the air and the flowers of the field.

Humanity's Role in Creation

Stewardship and Dominion

In Genesis 1:28, God gives humanity the mandate to "fill the earth and subdue it" and to "rule over" all living creatures. This dominion is not a license for exploitation but a call to stewardship. Humans are entrusted with the care and management of the earth, reflecting God's loving dominion. This stewardship involves nurturing and protecting the environment, ensuring the flourishing of all creation.

Co-Creators with God

As bearers of God's image, humans are also called to be co-creators with God. This creative partnership is an expression of love, as humans use their God-given abilities to cultivate, innovate, and enhance the world around them. In Genesis 2:15, Adam is placed in the Garden of Eden to "work it and take care of it," signifying humanity's role in co-creating with God. This creative work is an act of worship, reflecting God's creative love.

The Fall and Its Impact on Creation

The Disruption of Harmony

The entrance of sin into the world through the fall of Adam and Eve (Genesis 3) brought a disruption to the harmony of creation. This rebellion against God's loving rule resulted in broken relationships, both between humans and God and within creation itself. The ground is cursed, and pain and suffering become part of the human experience (Genesis 3:17-19). This brokenness affects all of creation, as Paul notes in Romans 8:22, where he describes creation as "groaning" in its bondage to decay.

God's Redemptive Plan

Despite the fall, God's love remains steadfast, and His redemptive plan unfolds throughout Scripture. God's commitment to restoring creation is an extension of His creative love. This redemptive narrative finds its climax in the person and work of Jesus Christ. In Colossians 1:19-20, Paul writes that through Christ, God is reconciling "all things" to Himself, "whether things on earth or things in heaven," making peace through Christ's blood shed on the cross. This cosmic reconciliation includes the restoration of creation itself.

The New Creation

The Promise of Renewal

The theme of new creation runs throughout the Bible, culminating in the vision of a renewed heaven and earth in Revelation 21-22. This eschatological hope is grounded in God's love and commitment to His creation. Revelation 21:1-4 depicts a new heaven and a new earth where God dwells with His people, wiping away every tear and abolishing death, mourning, crying, and pain. This renewed creation is a place of perfect harmony and flourishing, reflecting God's original intent.

Participation in the New Creation

Believers are called to participate in this new creation even now. In 2 Corinthians 5:17, Paul declares that "if anyone is in Christ, the new creation has come: The old has gone, the new is here!" This transformation is not merely individual but has cosmic implications. As followers of Christ, we are agents of this new creation, called to live out the values of the Kingdom of God and work towards the renewal of all things.

Practical Implications of Creation and Love

Environmental Stewardship

Understanding creation as an expression of God's love calls us to take seriously our role as stewards of the environment. This involves practical actions such as reducing waste, conserving resources, and advocating for policies that protect the natural world. Environmental stewardship is an act of love, reflecting our respect for God's creation and our commitment to its flourishing.

Promoting Justice and Equity

God's love for creation also calls us to promote justice and equity. This includes addressing issues such as poverty, inequality, and exploitation that harm both people and the environment. Working for justice is a way of participating in God's redemptive plan, reflecting His love for all creation.

Cultivating a Lifestyle of Gratitude and Worship

Recognizing creation as a gift of God's love inspires a lifestyle of gratitude and worship. This involves regularly acknowledging and giving thanks for the beauty and provision of creation. It also includes cultivating a sense of wonder and awe at God's creative work, leading us to worship Him more deeply.

God's love as the foundation of creation offers a profound understanding of the world and our place within it. From the act of creation to the ongoing work of redemption and the promise of a new creation, divine love is the thread that weaves through the entire narrative of Scripture. This understanding calls us to reflect God's love in our stewardship of the earth, our relationships with one another, and our worship of Him.

As we continue to explore the theology of love, let us be inspired by the love that undergirds creation. May we embrace our role as stewards and co-creators, working towards the flourishing of all creation and reflecting the love of the Creator in all we do.

## 1.3.0 HUMANITY CREATED IN THE IMAGE OF LOVING GOD

The doctrine that humanity is created in the image of God (imago Dei) is foundational to understanding human identity, dignity, and purpose. This concept is deeply intertwined with the nature of God's love, offering profound insights into what it means to be human and how we are to relate to God, each other, and the world. This chapter explores the implications of being created in the image of a loving God, emphasizing the transformative power of this divine image.

The Imago Dei: Understanding Our Divine Image

Biblical Foundation

The concept of humanity being created in God's image is introduced in the first chapter of Genesis: "So God created mankind in His own image, in the image of God He created them; male and female He created them" (Genesis 1:27). This verse highlights several key points:

- Both men and women are equally created in God's image.

- This divine image is intrinsic to human identity and purpose.

- The imago Dei sets humanity apart from the rest of creation.

The Nature of the Divine Image

Being made in the image of God encompasses several dimensions:

1. Relational: Just as God exists in a loving relationship within the Trinity, humans are designed for relationships. We are created to love and be loved, reflecting the relational nature of God.

2. Rational: Humans possess the ability to think, reason, and make moral choices. This rational capacity reflects God's wisdom and intentionality.

3. Creative: Humans are endowed with creativity, mirroring the Creator's ingenuity. Our ability to create art, music, literature, and technology is a reflection of God's creative spirit.

4. Moral: Humans have an innate sense of right and wrong, reflecting God's holiness and justice. This moral dimension calls us to live in a way that honors God's character.

### The Implications of the Imago Dei

### Intrinsic Worth and Dignity

Being created in the image of a loving God means that every human being has intrinsic worth and dignity. This understanding has profound implications for how we view ourselves and others. It challenges any form of dehumanization, discrimination, or violence. Each person, regardless of their status, abilities, or background, is valuable because they bear the image of God.

### A Call to Love

The imago Dei is fundamentally relational, calling us to love God and others. In Matthew 22:37-39, Jesus summarizes the greatest commandments: "Love the Lord your God with all your heart and with all your soul and with all your mind. This is the first and greatest commandment. And the second is like it: Love your neighbor as yourself." These commandments reflect the relational nature of the divine image. Our capacity to love is rooted in the fact that we are made in the image of a loving God.

Reflecting God's Character

As image-bearers, we are called to reflect God's character in the world. This includes embodying His love, justice, mercy, and truth. In Ephesians 5:1-2, Paul exhorts believers to "follow God's example, therefore, as dearly loved children and walk in the way of love, just as Christ loved us and gave Himself up for us as a fragrant offering and sacrifice to God." Reflecting God's character involves imitating the self-giving love of Christ.

The Fall and the Distortion of the Divine Image

The Impact of Sin

The entrance of sin into the world through the disobedience of Adam and Eve (Genesis 3) marred the divine image in humanity. Sin distorted our relationships with God, each other, and creation. The image of God in humanity was not obliterated, but it was tarnished. This distortion affects all aspects of human life, leading to brokenness, conflict, and suffering.

God's Redemptive Plan

Despite the fall, God's love remains steadfast, and His redemptive plan seeks to restore the divine image in humanity. This plan unfolds throughout Scripture, culminating in the life, death, and resurrection of Jesus Christ. In Christ, we see the perfect image of God (Colossians 1:15), who came to redeem and restore what was lost.

Restoration Through Christ

New Creation in Christ

In Christ, believers become a new creation. Paul writes in 2 Corinthians 5:17, "Therefore, if anyone is in Christ, the new creation has come: The old has gone, the new is here!" This transformation involves the restoration of the divine image within us. Through the work of the Holy Spirit, we are being renewed in the image of our Creator (Colossians 3:10).

Sanctification: Growing in the Likeness of Christ

The process of sanctification is the gradual restoration of the divine image as we grow in the likeness of Christ. This involves a transformation of character, where we increasingly reflect God's love, holiness, and righteousness. In Romans 8:29, Paul explains that God's purpose is for us to be "conformed to the image of His Son." This conformity is not about losing our individuality but about becoming the best version of ourselves as intended by God.

Living Out the Imago Dei

Loving God and Neighbor

Living out the imago Dei involves loving God with our whole being and loving our neighbor as ourselves. This love is not merely sentimental but is expressed through actions that seek the well-being of others. In 1 John 4:7-8, we are reminded that "love comes from God. Everyone who loves has been born of God and knows God. Whoever does not love does not know God, because God is love." Our ability to love is both a reflection of and a response to God's love.

Pursuing Justice and Compassion

Reflecting the image of a loving God also involves pursuing justice and showing compassion. This means standing against oppression, advocating for the marginalized, and working towards a more just and equitable society. Micah 6:8 encapsulates this call: "He has shown you, O mortal, what is good. And what does the Lord require of you? To act justly and to love mercy and to walk humbly with your God."

Stewarding Creation

As stewards of God's creation, we are called to care for the environment and use its resources responsibly. This stewardship reflects our respect for the Creator and our commitment to preserving the beauty and integrity of His creation. In Genesis 2:15, Adam is placed in the Garden of Eden "to work it and take care of it," signifying humanity's role in nurturing and protecting the earth.

### Building Community

The relational nature of the imago Dei calls us to build and nurture community. This involves creating spaces where people are valued, supported, and encouraged to flourish. The early church provides a model of such a community, as described in Acts 2:42-47, where believers shared life together, met each other's needs, and lived in harmony.

## The Ultimate Fulfillment of the Imago Dei

### The Eschatological Hope

The ultimate fulfillment of the imago Dei will be realized in the eschaton—the final consummation of all things. In Revelation 21:3-4, we see a vision of a new heaven and a new earth where God dwells with His people, and all things are made new. This renewed creation will be free from sin, suffering, and death, and humanity will perfectly reflect the image of God.

Understanding the eschatological hope of the imago Dei impacts how we live in the present. It gives us a perspective that transcends temporal struggles and suffering. Paul speaks of this hope in Romans 8:18-21, assuring us that "our present sufferings are not worth comparing with the glory that will be revealed in us." This hope empowers us to live boldly and love deeply, knowing that our ultimate destiny is to be fully conformed to the image of Christ.

Humanity being created in the image of a loving God is a foundational truth with profound implications for our identity, relationships, and purpose. The imago Dei bestows intrinsic worth and dignity upon every person, calling us to reflect God's love in our interactions with others and our stewardship of creation. Despite the distortion of sin, God's redemptive plan through Christ offers the hope of restoration and renewal.

As we continue our exploration of the theology of love, let us embrace our calling as image-bearers of a loving God. May we strive to reflect His character in all we do, working towards justice, compassion, and community, and living in the hope of the ultimate fulfillment of the imago Dei in the new creation.

# CHAPTER 02

## LOVE IN THE OLD TESTAMENT

2.1. Covenant Love

The Old Testament reveals God's love through His covenantal relationships with His people. Central to this revelation is the concept of hesed, often translated as "steadfast love" or "loving-kindness." This chapter explores the depth of hesed in the Old Testament and provides examples of God's covenantal love with Israel.

The Concept of Hesed (Steadfast Love) in the Old Testament

The Hebrew word hesed is rich and multifaceted, encompassing meanings such as steadfast love, mercy, loyalty, and kindness. Unlike the more general term for love, ahavah, hesed specifically denotes a committed and faithful love within the context of a covenant relationship. It implies a deep, enduring commitment that goes beyond mere emotion to include actions of kindness and loyalty.

Hesed is foundational to understanding God's character and His interactions with humanity. It is a love that is reliable, consistent, and enduring, reflecting God's unwavering commitment to His people.

Biblical Usage

The term hesed appears frequently in the Old Testament, often in contexts that highlight God's covenantal faithfulness. For example, in Exodus 34:6-7, God describes Himself to Moses: "The LORD, the LORD, the compassionate and gracious God, slow to anger, abounding in love (hesed) and faithfulness, maintaining love (hesed) to thousands, and forgiving wickedness, rebellion, and sin."

This self-revelation underscores the centrality of these in God's nature. It is not just an aspect of God's character but a defining quality of His relationship with His people.

Examples of God's Covenantal Love with Israel

The Abrahamic Covenant

God's covenant with Abraham marks the beginning of a special relationship with a chosen people. In Genesis 12:1-3, God calls Abraham to leave his country and promises to make him into a great nation, to bless him, and to bless all the families of the earth through him. This covenant, reaffirmed in Genesis 15 and 17, is an expression of God's hesed.

God's steadfast love is evident in His unwavering commitment to Abraham and his descendants, despite their shortcomings. For instance, in Genesis 17:7, God declares, "I will establish my covenant as an everlasting covenant between me and you and your descendants after you for the generations to come, to be your God and the God of your descendants after you." This everlasting covenant highlights God's enduring love and faithfulness.

The Mosaic Covenant

The Mosaic covenant, established at Mount Sinai, further illustrates God's hesed toward Israel. In Exodus 19:4-6, God reminds the Israelites of His deliverance from Egypt and calls them to be a "kingdom of priests and a holy nation." The giving of the Law, including the Ten Commandments, is a manifestation of God's love, providing guidance for living in a way that reflects His character.

God's hesed is also evident in His patience and mercy toward Israel's repeated disobedience. Despite their failures, God continually calls them back to Himself, exemplified in His dealings with them throughout their wilderness journey. In Deuteronomy 7:9, Moses reminds the people, "Know therefore that the LORD your God is God; He is the faithful God, keeping His covenant of love (hesed) to a thousand generations of those who love Him and keep His commandments."

The Davidic Covenant

The covenant with David is another profound example of God's hesed. In 2 Samuel 7:12-16, God promises David that his offspring will establish an everlasting kingdom. This covenant is reaffirmed in Psalm 89:1-4, where the psalmist celebrates God's steadfast love (hesed) and faithfulness to David and his descendants.

Despite David's sins, God's hesed remains steadfast. In 2 Samuel 12:13-14, after David's sin with Bathsheba, God forgives him but also disciplines him, demonstrating both His justice and His steadfast love. The promise of an everlasting kingdom is ultimately fulfilled in Jesus Christ, the Son of David, who establishes God's eternal reign.

The New Covenant Prophesied

The prophets also speak of a new covenant characterized by hesed. In Jeremiah 31:31-34, God promises a new covenant with Israel and Judah, one that involves the internalization of His law and the forgiveness of sins. This new covenant reflects God's enduring commitment to His people, despite their failures.

Ezekiel 36:24-28 similarly prophesies a renewed relationship between God and His people, marked by the giving of a new heart and spirit. This promise of restoration and renewal is a powerful testament to God's steadfast love.

### Theological Reflections on Hesed

### God's Unconditional Commitment

The concept of hesed highlights God's unconditional commitment to His people. Unlike human love, which can be fickle and conditional, God's hesed is steadfast and unwavering. It is a love that persists even in the face of unfaithfulness and rebellion. This divine love calls for a response of loyalty and faithfulness from God's people, reflecting the nature of the covenant relationship.

### Covenantal Faithfulness

God's hesed is intrinsically linked to His covenantal faithfulness. Throughout the Old Testament, God's actions toward Israel are governed by His covenant promises. Even when Israel breaks the covenant, God's hesed remains, offering hope and the possibility of restoration. This faithfulness is a cornerstone of Israel's identity and their relationship with God.

### A Model for Human Relationships

The hesed of God serves as a model for human relationships. Just as God shows steadfast love and loyalty to His people, so too are His people called to show hesed to one another. This involves acts of kindness, mercy, and faithfulness in our relationships, reflecting the character of God. In Micah 6:8, the prophet encapsulates this calling: "He has shown you, O mortal, what is good. And what does the LORD require of you? To act justly and to love mercy (hesed) and to walk humbly with your God."

Practical Implications of Hesed

Living Out Hesed in Daily Life

Understanding hesed calls us to embody steadfast love in our daily lives. This means committing to love others with the same loyalty and faithfulness that God shows us. It involves forgiveness, patience, and a willingness to bear with others in their weaknesses. Living out hesed requires intentionality and a deep commitment to loving others as God loves us.

Community and Covenant Relationships

Hesed also shapes our understanding of community and covenant relationships. In the context of the church, we are called to build communities marked by hesed, where members support and care for one another. This involves creating an environment of trust, accountability, and mutual encouragement. Covenant relationships, whether in marriage, family, or church, are to be characterized by steadfast love and faithfulness.

Social Justice and Mercy

The call to hesed extends to our engagement with society. Reflecting God's steadfast love involves advocating for justice and showing mercy to the marginalized and oppressed. It calls us to be agents of God's hesed in the world, working toward the flourishing of all people. This might involve supporting initiatives that promote social justice, caring for the poor, and standing against injustice.

The concept of hesed in the Old Testament reveals the depth and steadfastness of God's covenantal love. Through His relationships with Abraham, Moses, David, and the prophetic promises of a new covenant, we see a God who is unwavering in His commitment to His people. This divine hesed serves as both a foundation for our understanding of God's love and a model for how we are to love others.

As we continue our exploration of the theology of love, let us be inspired by the hesed of God. May we strive to embody this steadfast love in our relationships, our communities, and our engagement with the world, reflecting the enduring faithfulness and mercy of our covenant-keeping God.

## 2.2.0 LOVE IN THE LAW

The laws given to Israel through Moses form a significant part of the Old Testament, outlining how the people of God are to live in a relationship with Him and with one another. Central to these laws are the commandments to love God and neighbor, which serve as the foundation for ethical and moral conduct. This chapter delves into the commandment to love God and neighbor, exploring its significance, implications, and practical outworking in the lives of God's people.

The Commandment to Love God

The Shema: Deuteronomy 6:4-5

The commandment to love God is most clearly articulated in the Shema, a foundational Jewish prayer found in Deuteronomy 6:4-5: "Hear, O Israel: The LORD our God, the LORD is one. Love the LORD your God with all your heart and with all your soul and with all your strength." This commandment emphasizes total devotion to God, encompassing every aspect of one's being.

- Heart: In Hebrew thought, the heart represents the center of one's emotions, will, and intellect. To love God with all one's heart means to prioritize Him in every decision, desire, and thought. It signifies a heartfelt devotion that influences every part of life.

- Soul: The soul represents the essence of a person's life. Loving God with all one's soul involves a deep, personal commitment to God, integrating one's spiritual, emotional, and physical existence.

- Strength: Loving God with all one's strength implies using all resources, abilities, and energy to serve and honor God. It calls for a love that manifests in action, dedication, and perseverance.

The command to love God is given within the context of the covenant relationship between God and Israel. This covenant is marked by God's steadfast love and faithfulness, as seen in His acts of deliverance and provision. In response, Israel is called to love God wholeheartedly, reflecting their gratitude and allegiance to Him.

Teaching and Remembering

Deuteronomy 6:6-9 emphasizes the importance of internalizing and transmitting this commandment: "These commandments that I give you today are to be on your hearts. Impress them on your children. Talk about them when you sit at home and when you walk along the road, when you lie down and when you get up. Tie them as symbols on your hands and bind them on your foreheads. Write them on the doorframes of your houses and on your gates."

This passage underscores the need for continuous remembrance and teaching of God's commandments. It highlights the importance of integrating the love of God into daily life and family practices, ensuring that future generations understand and embrace this foundational command.

The Commandment to Love Neighbor

Leviticus 19:18

The commandment to love one's neighbor is articulated in Leviticus 19:18: "Do not seek revenge or bear a grudge against anyone among your people, but love your neighbor as yourself. I am the LORD." This commandment emphasizes the importance of love in interpersonal relationships, calling for an ethic of care, forgiveness, and mutual respect.

The Holiness Code

Leviticus 19 is part of the Holiness Code, which outlines practical applications of holiness in the daily lives of the Israelites. The command to love one's neighbor is integral to living a holy life, reflecting God's character in human relationships. This love is not limited to feelings but is expressed through actions that promote the well-being of others.

Practical Expressions of Neighborly Love

The surrounding verses in Leviticus 19 provide specific examples of what it means to love one's neighbor:

- Justice and Fairness: "Do not pervert justice; do not show partiality to the poor or favoritism to the great, but judge your neighbor fairly" (Leviticus 19:15). Loving one's neighbor involves treating others with justice and impartiality.

- Care for the Vulnerable: "Do not curse the deaf or put a stumbling block in front of the blind, but fear your God. I am the LORD" (Leviticus 19:14). This command emphasizes the need to protect and care for the vulnerable and marginalized.

- Honesty and Integrity: "Do not deceive one another" (Leviticus 19:11). Loving one's neighbor includes honesty, transparency, and integrity in all dealings.

The Broader Context

While Leviticus 19:18 specifically addresses interpersonal relationships within the community of Israel, the broader biblical narrative expands the concept of neighbor to include all people. This is exemplified in the teachings of Jesus, who reaffirms and broadens these commandments.

Jesus' Affirmation and Expansion

The Greatest Commandments

In the New Testament, Jesus affirms the centrality of these commandments. When asked about the greatest commandment, Jesus replies, "'Love the Lord your God with all your heart and with all your soul and with all your mind.' This is the first and greatest commandment. And the second is like it: 'Love your neighbor as yourself.' All the Law and the Prophets hang on these two commandments" (Matthew 22:37-40).

By linking these two commandments, Jesus highlights their inseparable nature. Loving God and loving neighbor are fundamentally connected, forming the basis for all other commandments.

The Parable of the Good Samaritan

In Luke 10:25-37, Jesus expands the understanding of who is considered a neighbor through the Parable of the Good Samaritan. When a lawyer asks, "And who is my neighbor?" Jesus responds with a story that challenges social and ethnic boundaries. The Samaritan, who is traditionally viewed as an enemy, demonstrates love by caring for the wounded man.

This parable underscores that neighborly love transcends social, ethnic, and religious divisions. It calls for compassion and action toward anyone in need, reflecting the universal nature of God's love.

Theological Reflections on Love in the Law

Covenantal Relationship

The commandments to love God and neighbor are rooted in the covenantal relationship between God and His people. This relationship is characterized by mutual commitment, faithfulness, and love. God's commandments are not arbitrary rules but expressions of His loving nature, intended to guide His people in living lives that reflect His character.

Ethics and Worship

Loving God and neighbor integrates ethics and worship. True worship is not confined to religious rituals but is lived out through ethical behavior and loving relationships. The prophets often emphasize that God desires mercy, justice, and humility more than ritual sacrifices (Hosea 6:6, Micah 6:8).

Holistic Love

The commandments to love God and neighbor call for holistic love that encompasses the whole person—heart, soul, mind, and strength. This love is comprehensive, affecting every aspect of life and every relationship. It calls for a love that is both vertical (toward God) and horizontal (toward others).

Practical Implications of Love in the Law

Personal Devotion

Loving God with all our heart, soul, and strength involves cultivating a personal relationship with Him through prayer, study of Scripture, and obedience. It requires a commitment to align our desires, thoughts, and actions with God's will.

Community and Social Responsibility

Loving our neighbor as ourselves involves actively seeking the well-being of others. This includes practical acts of kindness, advocacy for justice, and fostering inclusive and supportive communities. It challenges us to break down barriers and extend love to all people, regardless of differences.

Holistic Living

Integrating the love of God and neighbor into daily life requires intentionality and consistency. It involves making ethical choices that reflect our love for God and others, whether in our personal lives, workplaces, or broader society.

The commandments to love God and neighbor are central to the Old Testament Law and are reaffirmed and expanded by Jesus in the New Testament. These commandments reflect the heart of God's covenantal relationship with His people, calling for a holistic love that integrates worship, ethics, and community.

As we continue to explore the theology of love, let us be inspired by these foundational commandments. May we strive to love God with all our heart, soul, mind, and strength, and to love our neighbors as ourselves, reflecting the steadfast love of God in every aspect of our lives.

## 2.2.1 THE ROLE OF LOVE IN THE MOSAIC LAW

The Mosaic Law, given to the Israelites through Moses, is a comprehensive guide for living that encompasses various aspects of life, including moral, ceremonial, and civil laws. At the heart of this legal code is the centrality of love— love for God and love for neighbor. This chapter explores the role of love in the Mosaic Law, highlighting how it shapes the ethical and communal life of God's people.

The Foundation of the Mosaic Law

The Giving of the Law

The Mosaic Law, encapsulated in the Torah, represents God's covenantal relationship with Israel. Following the Israelites' deliverance from Egypt, God establishes this covenant at Mount Sinai, providing the Ten Commandments as the core moral framework (Exodus 20:1-17). The Law is further expanded with detailed instructions covering various aspects of life, aimed at creating a holy and just society.

The Purpose of the Law

The purpose of the Mosaic Law is to guide the Israelites to live in accordance with God's will. It serves as a means to maintain their distinct identity as God's chosen people and to reflect His character in their communal and personal lives. Central to this purpose is the principle of love, which undergirds all commandments and regulations.

Love for God in the Mosaic Law

The Shema: Deuteronomy 6:4-5

The Shema, found in Deuteronomy 6:4-5, is the foundational declaration of Israel's faith and the primary commandment regarding the love of God: "Hear, O Israel: The LORD our God, the LORD is one. Love the LORD your God with all your heart and with all your soul and with all your strength." This commandment calls for total devotion to God, encompassing every aspect of a person's being.

Total Devotion

Loving God with all one's heart, soul, and strength means prioritizing Him above all else. It involves a holistic commitment that integrates worship, obedience, and everyday actions. The Mosaic Law provides practical ways to express this love, such as observing the Sabbath, offering sacrifices, and following dietary laws.

Remembrance and Teaching

The Mosaic Law emphasizes the importance of remembering and teaching God's commandments. Deuteronomy 6:6-9 instructs the Israelites to keep these commands in their hearts, teach them to their children, and incorporate them into their daily lives. This practice ensures that the love of God remains central to their identity and way of life.

Love for Neighbor in the Mosaic Law

Leviticus 19:18

The commandment to love one's neighbor as oneself is explicitly stated in Leviticus 19:18: "Do not seek revenge or bear a grudge against anyone among your people, but love your neighbor as yourself. I am the LORD." This commandment highlights the ethical and relational dimensions of the Mosaic Law.

Justice and Fairness

The Mosaic Law contains numerous provisions aimed at ensuring justice and fairness in society. For example, Leviticus 19:15 instructs, "Do not pervert justice; do not show partiality to the poor or favoritism to the great, but judge your neighbor fairly." Loving one's neighbor involves treating others with equity and impartiality.

Care for the Vulnerable

The Law includes specific commands to protect and care for the vulnerable, such as the poor, widows, orphans, and foreigners. Leviticus 19:9-10 instructs landowners to leave the gleanings of their harvest for the poor and the foreigners. This provision reflects God's concern for the marginalized and calls the community to extend love and compassion.

Honesty and Integrity

The Mosaic Law emphasizes the importance of honesty and integrity in relationships. Leviticus 19:11 states, "Do not steal. Do not lie. Do not deceive one another." Loving one's neighbor involves being truthful and trustworthy, and fostering a community based on mutual respect and reliability.

The Interconnection of Love for God and Neighbor

The Greatest Commandments

Jesus highlights the interconnection of loving God and neighbor in the New Testament. When asked about the greatest commandment, He replies, "'Love the Lord your God with all your heart and with all your soul and with all your mind.' This is the first and greatest commandment. And the second is like it: 'Love your neighbor as yourself.' All the Law and the Prophets hang on these two commandments" (Matthew 22:37-40).

Holistic Love

The Mosaic Law integrates the love of God and neighbor into a holistic framework. Loving God is expressed through obedience to His commands, which include ethical treatment of others. Conversely, genuine love for one's neighbor flows from a heart devoted to God. This holistic approach ensures that worship and ethics are inseparable, fostering a community that reflects God's love and justice.

The Practical Outworking of Love in the Mosaic Law

Rituals and Ceremonies

The Mosaic Law includes rituals and ceremonies that express love for God. These practices, such as sacrifices and festivals, provide tangible ways for the Israelites to demonstrate their devotion and gratitude. They also serve as communal expressions of faith, fostering unity and shared identity.

Social and Economic Practices

The Law also addresses social and economic practices, ensuring that love for neighbor is manifested in everyday life. For instance, the Sabbath year and the Year of Jubilee (Leviticus 25) provide economic relief and promote social equality. These practices prevent the accumulation of wealth and power in the hands of a few, ensuring that everyone has the opportunity to thrive.

Legal Protections

Legal protections in the Mosaic Law reflect the principle of love for neighbor. Provisions for fair trials, protection of property rights, and restitution for wrongs committed ensure that justice is upheld. These laws create a framework for a just society where individuals are treated with dignity and respect.

Theological Reflections on Love in the Mosaic Law

God's Character Reflected in the Law

The Mosaic Law reflects God's character, particularly His love, justice, and holiness. By following the Law, the Israelites embody these divine attributes, serving as a testimony to the nations. The Law is not merely a set of rules but a revelation of God's nature and His desire for a loving and just community.

The Law as a Tutor

Paul describes the Law as a tutor that leads us to Christ (Galatians 3:24). The Mosaic Law, with its emphasis on love for God and neighbor, prepares the way for the fuller revelation of love in Jesus Christ. It teaches the fundamental principles of love and justice, which are fully realized in the life and teachings of Jesus.

A Call to Holiness

The Mosaic Law calls God's people to holiness, set apart by their love and ethical conduct. This holiness is not an abstract concept but is demonstrated through practical acts of love and justice. The Law provides a blueprint for living a life that reflects God's holiness and love.

Practical Implications of Love in the Mosaic Law

Personal Devotion and Obedience

Loving God through the Law involves personal devotion and obedience. This includes regular practices of worship, prayer, and study of Scripture. It also means aligning one's life with God's commandments and striving to live in a way that honors Him.

Community Building

Loving one's neighbor through the Law involves actively building and nurturing a community. This includes acts of kindness, support for the vulnerable, and efforts to promote justice and equality. It calls for a commitment to fostering relationships based on love, respect, and mutual support.

Advocacy and Social Justice

The principles of love in the Mosaic Law call for advocacy and action for social justice. This involves standing against injustice, supporting the marginalized, and working towards systemic changes that reflect God's love and justice.

It requires a commitment to creating a society where all people are treated with dignity and respect.

The role of love in the Mosaic Law is central to understanding the ethical and communal life of God's people. The commandments to love God and neighbor provide the foundation for the entire legal framework, integrating worship, ethics, and community. This holistic approach reflects God's character and His desire for a loving and just society.

As we continue to explore the theology of love, let us be inspired by the Mosaic Law's emphasis on love. May we strive to love God with all our heart, soul, mind, and strength, and to love our neighbors as ourselves, embodying the principles of love and justice in every aspect of our lives.

## 2.3.0 PROPHETS AND LOVE

The prophetic literature of the Old Testament is replete with calls to return to God's love. The prophets, acting as God's messengers, continually urged the people of Israel to repent from their waywardness and embrace the steadfast love of God. This chapter explores how the prophets communicated God's love and the urgent call to return to a covenantal relationship with Him.

The prophets were chosen by God to deliver His messages to the people of Israel and Judah. Their primary role was to call the people back to faithfulness and obedience to God. This often involved confronting sin, warning of impending judgment, and offering hope for restoration.

Central to the prophetic message was the reminder of the covenantal relationship between God and Israel. The prophets emphasized that this covenant was based on God's hesed—His steadfast love and faithfulness. Despite the people's unfaithfulness, God's love remained constant, and His desire for their return was relentless.

Prophetic Calls to Return to God's Love

Hosea: Love and Faithfulness

The prophet Hosea's ministry vividly illustrates God's enduring love. Hosea's personal life, including his marriage to Gomer, serves as a metaphor for God's relationship with Israel. Despite Gomer's unfaithfulness, Hosea is commanded to love her, reflecting God's steadfast love for His wayward people.

- Hosea 2:19-20: "I will betroth you to me forever; I will betroth you in righteousness and justice, in love and compassion. I will betroth you in faithfulness, and you will acknowledge the LORD." These verses capture God's promise to restore the broken relationship and renew His covenant with Israel, emphasizing His enduring love and compassion.

Jeremiah: Call to Repentance

Jeremiah, known as the "weeping prophet," delivered a poignant message of both judgment and hope. His prophecies often highlighted the people's infidelity and the consequences of their actions but also conveyed God's deep love and desire for their repentance.

- Jeremiah 31:3: "The LORD appeared to us in the past, saying: 'I have loved you with an everlasting love; I have drawn you with unfailing kindness.'" This declaration underscores God's unwavering love and His persistent call for Israel to return to Him.

- Jeremiah 3:12-14: "Return, faithless Israel,' declares the LORD, 'I will frown on you no longer, for I am faithful,' declares the LORD, 'I will not be angry forever. Only acknowledge your guilt—you have rebelled against the LORD your God...Return, faithless people,' declares the LORD, 'for I am your husband. I will choose you—one from a town and two from a clan—and bring you to Zion.'" Here, God's call to repentance is coupled with a promise of restoration, reflecting His covenantal love.

Isaiah: A Vision of Restoration

Isaiah's prophecies span themes of judgment, comfort, and future glory. He vividly portrays God's holiness and the people's sinfulness, but he also offers profound visions of hope and restoration based on God's love.

- Isaiah 54:10: "Though the mountains be shaken and the hills be removed, yet my unfailing love for you will not be shaken nor my covenant of peace be removed,' says the LORD, who has compassion on you." This verse emphasizes the unshakeable nature of God's love and His commitment to His people.

- Isaiah 49:15-16: "Can a mother forget the baby at her breast and have no compassion on the child she has borne? Though she may forget, I will not forget you! See, I have engraved you on the palms of my hands; your walls are ever before me." This tender imagery portrays God's deep, parental love and His enduring remembrance of His people.

Ezekiel: Heart Transformation

Ezekiel's ministry occurred during the Babylonian exile, and his messages often addressed the people's idolatry and rebellion. Yet, amidst the warnings, Ezekiel also conveyed God's promise of a renewed relationship based on His steadfast love.

- Ezekiel 36:26-28: "I will give you a new heart and put a new spirit in you; I will remove from you your heart of stone and give you a heart of flesh. And I will put my Spirit in you and move you to follow my decrees and be careful to keep my laws. Then you will live in the land I gave your ancestors; you will be my people, and I will be your God." This promise of heart transformation and the indwelling of God's Spirit signifies a deep renewal rooted in divine love.

Amos: Justice and Righteousness

Amos, a prophet of social justice, emphasized that true worship of God must be accompanied by justice and righteousness in society. His messages often condemned the exploitation and oppression of the poor, calling the people to embody God's love in their treatment of others.

- Amos 5:24: "But let justice roll on like a river, righteousness like a never-failing stream!" This call for justice and righteousness reflects God's character and His desire for a society that mirrors His love and equity.

The Theological Significance of Prophetic Love

God's Relentless Pursuit

The prophetic calls to return to God's love highlight His relentless pursuit of His people. Despite their repeated unfaithfulness, God's love remains steadfast, and He continuously invites them back into a covenantal relationship. This relentless pursuit underscores the depth and persistence of God's love.

Judgment and Hope

The prophets often balanced messages of judgment with promises of hope and restoration. While they did not shy away from confronting sin and its consequences, they also conveyed God's unwavering love and His plans for renewal. This balance reflects the nature of divine love, which is both just and merciful.

Covenantal Faithfulness

The prophetic messages reinforce the theme of covenantal faithfulness. God's love is not contingent on Israel's faithfulness but is rooted in His covenantal commitment. This faithfulness calls the people to respond with repentance, obedience, and a renewed commitment to their relationship with God.

The prophetic calls to return to God's love emphasize the importance of repentance and renewal in our own lives. This involves acknowledging our shortcomings, turning away from sin, and embracing God's love and forgiveness. It calls for a continuous process of spiritual renewal and transformation.

Social Justice and Compassion

The prophetic emphasis on justice and righteousness challenges us to reflect God's love in our treatment of others. This involves advocating for justice, showing compassion to the marginalized, and working towards a society that reflects God's love and equity.

Faithfulness in Relationships

The prophets' messages highlight the importance of faithfulness in our relationships with God and others. This involves cultivating a deep, personal relationship with God through prayer, worship, and obedience. It also calls for integrity, loyalty, and compassion in our relationships with others.

The prophetic calls to return to God's love are a powerful testament to His steadfast and relentless love for His people. The messages of prophets like Hosea, Jeremiah, Isaiah, Ezekiel, and Amos emphasize the depth of God's love, His desire for a renewed relationship, and the call to embody His love in our lives.

As we continue to explore the theology of love, let us be inspired by the prophetic vision of a loving and just relationship with God and others. May we heed the prophetic call to return to God's love, embody His compassion and justice, and live faithfully in our covenantal relationship with Him.

## 2.3.1 THE PORTRAYAL OF GOD'S PASSIONATE LOVE FOR HIS PEOPLE

The Old Testament prophets vividly portray God's passionate love for His people through powerful imagery, poignant messages, and heartfelt appeals. This chapter explores how the prophets depict God's ardent love, highlighting the depth of His affection and His relentless pursuit of a restored relationship with Israel.

Hosea: The Unfailing Love of a Faithful Husband

The book of Hosea uniquely captures God's passionate love through the metaphor of marriage. God commands Hosea to marry Gomer, a woman who is unfaithful, to illustrate Israel's unfaithfulness to Him (Hosea 1:2). Despite Gomer's infidelity, Hosea's steadfast love and commitment to her symbolize God's unwavering love for Israel.

Hosea's prophecies reveal God's profound heartache over Israel's betrayal, yet they also convey His hopeful longing for reconciliation. In Hosea 2:14-20, God speaks tenderly of wooing Israel back to Him:

"Therefore, I am now going to allure her; I will lead her into the wilderness and speak tenderly to her. ... 'In that day,' declares the LORD, 'you will call me "my husband"; you will no longer call me "my master." ... I will betroth you to me forever; I will betroth you in righteousness and justice, in love and compassion. I will betroth you in faithfulness, and you will acknowledge the LORD.'"

This passage vividly portrays God's passionate desire to restore the broken relationship, emphasizing His love, compassion, and faithfulness.

Jeremiah: The Everlasting Love of a Caring Father

Jeremiah often portrays God as a loving father yearning for His wayward children to return. This father-child metaphor underscores the deep emotional bond and enduring commitment God has toward Israel.

In Jeremiah 31:3, God declares, "I have loved you with an everlasting love; I have drawn you with unfailing kindness." This statement highlights the eternal and unchanging nature of God's love, which persists despite Israel's repeated rebellion.

Jeremiah's prophecies are filled with promises of restoration, reflecting God's passionate commitment to His people. In Jeremiah 29:11-14, God assures His people of a hopeful future:

"'For I know the plans I have for you,' declares the LORD, 'plans to prosper you and not to harm you, plans to give you hope and a future. Then you will call on me and come and pray to me, and I will listen to you. You will seek me and find me when you seek me with all your heart. I will be found by you,' declares the LORD, 'and will bring you back from captivity.'"

These promises reveal God's longing to bless His people and restore their fortunes, driven by His passionate love and desire for their well-being.

Isaiah: The Comforting Love of a Redeeming Savior

Isaiah's prophecies often highlight God's comforting love, particularly during times of distress and exile. In Isaiah 40:1-2, God speaks words of comfort to His people:

"Comfort, comfort my people, says your God. Speak tenderly to Jerusalem, and proclaim to her that her hard service has been completed, that her sin has been paid for, that she has received from the LORD's hand double for all her sins."

This passage emphasizes God's compassion and His desire to bring comfort and healing to His people.

Isaiah also introduces the concept of the Suffering Servant, a messianic figure who embodies God's redeeming love through self-sacrifice. Isaiah 53:4-5 describes this servant's suffering on behalf of the people:

"Surely he took up our pain and bore our suffering, yet we considered him punished by God, stricken by him, and afflicted. But he was pierced for our transgressions, he was crushed for our iniquities; the punishment that brought us peace was on him, and by his wounds, we are healed."

This prophecy foreshadows the ultimate demonstration of God's passionate love through the sacrificial death of Jesus Christ, who bears the sins of humanity to bring about reconciliation and healing.

Ezekiel: The Transforming Love of a Restoring God

Ezekiel's prophecies convey God's relentless pursuit of His people, even in their deepest rebellion. In Ezekiel 16, God uses the metaphor of an unfaithful wife to describe Israel's infidelity, yet He also declares His unwavering commitment to restore her:

"'Yet I will remember the covenant I made with you in the days of your youth, and I will establish an everlasting covenant with you. ... So I will establish my covenant with you, and you will know that I am the LORD. Then, when I make atonement for you for all you have done, you will remember and be ashamed and never again open your mouth because of your humiliation,' declares the Sovereign LORD" (Ezekiel 16:60, 62-63).

This passage underscores God's passionate love that seeks to renew and transform His people, restoring them to a right relationship with Him.

Ezekiel also prophesies about the internal transformation that God's love will bring. In Ezekiel 36:26-28, God promises to give His people a new heart and spirit:

"I will give you a new heart and put a new spirit in you; I will remove from you your heart of stone and give you a heart of flesh. And I will put my Spirit in you and move you to follow my decrees and be careful to keep my laws. Then you will live in the land I gave your ancestors; you will be my people, and I will be your God."

This promise reflects God's passionate desire to transform His people from within, enabling them to live in accordance with His will.

Zephaniah: The Joyful Love of a Singing God

The book of Zephaniah provides a unique portrayal of God's love, depicting Him as a joyful, singing deity who delights in His people. Zephaniah 3:17 states:

"The LORD your God is with you, the Mighty Warrior who saves. He will take great delight in you; in His love He will no longer rebuke you, but will rejoice over you with singing."

This imagery captures the exuberant and joyful nature of God's love, emphasizing His delight in His people and His desire to celebrate their relationship.

Theological Reflections on God's Passionate Love

The prophets vividly portray God's love as unconditional and persistent. Despite Israel's repeated failures and unfaithfulness, God's love remains steadfast. This divine love is not based on the people's merit but on God's unwavering commitment to His covenant.

God's passionate love always seeks restoration and reconciliation. The prophetic messages consistently convey God's desire to restore the broken relationship with His people, offering forgiveness and renewal. This love is both just and merciful, addressing sin while providing a path to healing and wholeness.

The passionate love of God as depicted by the prophets serves as a model for human relationships. It challenges us to love others with the same steadfastness, compassion, and desire for restoration. This divine love calls us to go beyond mere feelings and to engage in actions that reflect God's transformative and redemptive love.

Practical Implications of God's Passionate Love

Understanding God's passionate love invites us to embrace it fully in our own lives. This involves recognizing and accepting God's unwavering commitment to us, despite our flaws and failures. It calls for a deep, personal relationship with God, grounded in His love and faithfulness.

We are called to reflect God's passionate love in our relationships with others. This includes showing steadfast love, forgiveness, and compassion, even in the face of betrayal or hurt. It involves actively seeking the well-being and restoration of those around us, embodying the love that God has shown us.

God's passionate love calls us to build communities characterized by love, justice, and compassion. This involves advocating for the marginalized, promoting reconciliation, and creating environments where people can experience the transforming power of God's love. It challenges us to be agents of God's love in our churches, neighborhoods, and broader society.

The portrayal of God's passionate love for His people in the prophetic literature of the Old Testament is a powerful testament to the depth and persistence of divine love. Through vivid metaphors and heartfelt messages, the prophets convey God's unwavering commitment to His people and His relentless pursuit of a restored relationship.

As we continue to explore the theology of love, let us be inspired by the passionate love of God as depicted by the prophets. May we embrace this love in our own lives, reflect it in our relationships, and live out its transformative power in our communities, embodying the steadfast and redemptive love of our faithful God.

# CHAPTER 03

---

## LOVE IN THE NEW TESTAMENT
### 3.1. The Love of Christ

The New Testament reveals the love of God most profoundly through the person and work of Jesus Christ. Central to this revelation is the Incarnation, where God becomes flesh in the person of Jesus. This act of divine condescension, encapsulated in John 3:16, is the ultimate expression of God's love. This chapter explores the Incarnation as the pinnacle of God's love, examining its theological significance and practical implications for believers.

The Incarnation: God Becomes Flesh

John 3:16: The Heart of the Gospel

John 3:16 is one of the most well-known and beloved verses in the Bible: "For God so loved the world that He gave His one and only Son, that whoever believes in Him shall not perish but have eternal life." This verse succinctly captures the essence of the Gospel—the profound love of God manifested in the giving of His Son, Jesus Christ.

The Incarnation is the mystery of God becoming human in the person of Jesus Christ. In John 1:14, we read, "The Word became flesh and made His dwelling among us. We have seen His glory, the glory of the one and only Son, who came from the Father, full of grace and truth." The Word, who was with God and was God (John 1:1), takes on human nature and lives among us. This act of divine humility and solidarity with humanity is a profound demonstration of God's love.

Theological Significance of the Incarnation

The Incarnation signifies God's solidarity with humanity. By taking on human flesh, God enters into the full human experience, including suffering, temptation, and death. This solidarity is an expression of God's love, demonstrating His willingness to enter into our brokenness and to redeem it from within.

Revealing the Father

In the Incarnation, Jesus reveals the Father to us. In John 14:9, Jesus says, "Anyone who has seen me has seen the Father." Through His life, teachings, and actions, Jesus provides a tangible and visible representation of God's character and love. He embodies God's grace, truth, compassion, and righteousness, offering a clear picture of who God is and how much He loves us.

The Perfect Mediator

As both fully God and fully human, Jesus serves as the perfect mediator between God and humanity. In 1 Timothy 2:5, Paul writes, "For there is one God and one mediator between God and mankind, the man Christ Jesus." Through His Incarnation, Jesus bridges the gap created by sin, making it possible for us to be reconciled to God.

The Love of Christ in His Ministry

Throughout His earthly ministry, Jesus exemplifies God's love through acts of healing and compassion. He reaches out to the marginalized, the sick, and the outcasts, demonstrating that God's love is inclusive and transformative. In Matthew 9:36, we read, "When He saw the crowds, He had compassion on them, because they were harassed and helpless, like sheep without a shepherd." Jesus' compassion reflects the heart of God, who is deeply concerned for the well-being of His people.

Teaching and Discipleship

Jesus' teachings are infused with the message of God's love. The Sermon on the Mount (Matthew 5-7) provides a radical vision of God's kingdom, characterized by love, mercy, and justice. Jesus teaches His disciples to love their enemies, to forgive, and to seek first the kingdom of God. His parables often illustrate the depth of God's love, such as the Parable of the Prodigal Son (Luke 15:11-32), which portrays a father's unconditional love and forgiveness.

Sacrificial Love

The ultimate demonstration of Christ's love is found in His sacrificial death on the cross. In John 15:13, Jesus states, "Greater love has no one than this: to lay down one's life for one's friends." Jesus willingly lays down His life to atone for the sins of humanity, offering Himself as the perfect sacrifice. This act of sacrificial love fulfills God's redemptive plan and provides the means for our salvation.

The Cross: The Pinnacle of God's Love

The cross is the pinnacle of God's love, where Jesus atones for the sins of the world and reconciles humanity to God. In Romans 5:8, Paul writes, "But God demonstrates His own love for us in this: While we were still sinners, Christ died for us." The cross reveals the extent of God's love, as He bears the punishment for our sins and restores the broken relationship between God and humanity.

Victory Over Sin and Death

Through His death and resurrection, Jesus conquers sin and death, securing eternal life for all who believe in Him. In 1 Corinthians 15:55-57, Paul declares, "Where, O death, is your victory? Where, O death, is your sting? ... But thanks be to God! He gives us the victory through our Lord Jesus Christ." The resurrection is the ultimate victory of love over the forces of evil and death, offering hope and assurance to believers.

The Practical Implications of the Incarnation

Understanding the Incarnation and the love of Christ calls us to live in the light of God's love. This involves embracing our identity as beloved children of God and allowing His love to transform every aspect of our lives. In 1 John 4:16, we read, "God is love. Whoever lives in love lives in God, and God in them." Living in God's love means cultivating a deep, personal relationship with Him and reflecting His love in our actions and relationships.

Loving Others as Christ Loved Us

Jesus' commandment to His disciples is clear: "A new command I give you: Love one another. As I have loved you, so you must love one another" (John 13:34). The Incarnation and the sacrificial love of Christ set the standard for how we are to love others. This love is selfless, unconditional, and transformative. It calls us to serve, forgive, and seek the well-being of others, following the example of Christ.

Embodied Witness

The Incarnation underscores the importance of embodied witness—living out our faith in tangible ways. Just as Jesus embodied God's love through His actions, we are called to be His hands and feet in the world. This involves acts of compassion, justice, and service, demonstrating God's love to those around us. In Matthew 25:40, Jesus teaches that whatever we do for the least of these, we do for Him, highlighting the significance of practical expressions of love.

The Hope of the Incarnation

The Presence of God with Us

The Incarnation assures us of God's continual presence with us. In Matthew 28:20, Jesus promises, "And surely I am with you always, to the very end of the age." This promise provides comfort and strength, knowing that we are never alone. God's love is ever-present, guiding and sustaining us through all circumstances.

The Promise of Eternal Life

The Incarnation also offers the hope of eternal life. Through faith in Jesus, we are granted the gift of eternal life and the promise of a future resurrection. In John 11:25-26, Jesus declares, "I am the resurrection and the life. The one who believes in me will live, even though they die; and whoever lives by believing in me will never die." This hope transforms our perspective on life and death, giving us confidence in the enduring love of God.

The Incarnation is the ultimate expression of God's love, revealing His profound solidarity with humanity and His desire for our redemption and reconciliation. Through the life, teachings, sacrificial death, and resurrection of Jesus Christ, we witness the depth of God's love and the lengths to which He will go to restore us to Himself.

As we continue to explore the theology of love, let us be deeply moved by the love of Christ. May we embrace His love in our own lives, reflect it in our relationships, and live out its transformative power in the world. The Incarnation calls us to a higher standard of love, one that is selfless, sacrificial, and redemptive, embodying the very heart of God.

## 3.1.0 THE LOVE OF CHRIST

The teachings of Jesus provide a profound and transformative understanding of love, central to which is the Sermon on the Mount. This sermon encapsulates Jesus' radical vision for how His followers are to embody love in their daily lives. This chapter delves into Jesus' teachings on love, examining key aspects from the Sermon on the Mount and other significant passages in the Gospels.

The Sermon on the Mount: A Radical Vision of Love

The Sermon on the Mount, found in Matthew chapters 5-7, is one of the most comprehensive collections of Jesus' teachings. It begins with the Beatitudes, which outline the characteristics and blessings of those who follow God's ways. The sermon then addresses various aspects of life, offering a radical reinterpretation of the Law that centers on love and righteousness.

The Beatitudes: The Heart of the Kingdom

The Beatitudes (Matthew 5:3-12) describe the attitudes and qualities that characterize the citizens of God's Kingdom. They emphasize humility, mercy, peacemaking, and a thirst for righteousness. These qualities reflect the heart of love that Jesus calls His followers to embody:

- Blessed are the poor in spirit, for theirs is the kingdom of heaven.

- Blessed are those who mourn, for they will be comforted.

- Blessed are the meek, for they will inherit the earth.

- Blessed are those who hunger and thirst for righteousness, for they will be filled.

- Blessed are the merciful, for they will be shown mercy.

- Blessed are the pure in heart, for they will see God.

- Blessed are the peacemakers, for they will be called children of God.

- Blessed are those who are persecuted because of righteousness, for theirs is the kingdom of heaven.

These declarations underscore the values of God's Kingdom, which are rooted in love and counter to the world's values of power and self-interest.

Love Your Enemies

One of the most challenging and radical aspects of Jesus' teachings on love is the command to love one's enemies. In Matthew 5:43-48, Jesus says:

"You have heard that it was said, 'Love your neighbor and hate your enemy.' But I tell you, love your enemies and pray for those who persecute you, that you may be children of your Father in heaven. He causes His sun to rise on the evil and the good, and sends rain on the righteous and the unrighteous. If you love those who love you, what reward will you get? Are not even the tax collectors doing that? And if you greet only your own people, what are you doing more than others? Do not even pagans do that? Be perfect, therefore, as your heavenly Father is perfect."

This teaching extends the concept of love beyond the familiar and comfortable, challenging followers of Jesus to exhibit a love that mirrors God's impartial and unconditional love. Loving enemies involves seeking their well-being, praying for them, and responding to hostility with grace and forgiveness.

Turning the Other Cheek

In Matthew 5:38-42, Jesus further expands on how to respond to mistreatment:

"You have heard that it was said, 'Eye for eye, and tooth for tooth.' But I tell you, do not resist an evil person. If anyone slaps you on the right cheek, turn to them the other cheek also. And if anyone wants to sue you and take your shirt, hand over your coat as well. If anyone forces you to go one mile, go with them two miles. Give to the one who asks you, and do not turn away from the one who wants to borrow from you."

These instructions call for a radical response to injustice and personal injury. Instead of seeking retaliation, Jesus urges His followers to respond with generosity and love, breaking the cycle of violence and demonstrating the transformative power of love.

The Golden Rule

In Matthew 7:12, Jesus encapsulates His ethical teachings in what is commonly known as the Golden Rule: "So in everything, do to others what you would have them do to you, for this sums up the Law and the Prophets." This principle calls for empathy and proactive love, treating others with the same respect and kindness that we desire for ourselves. It summarizes the ethical demands of the Mosaic Law and the prophetic writings, centering them on love and mutual respect.

Jesus' teachings emphasize that true righteousness goes beyond external compliance with the Law to include internal attitudes and intentions. In Matthew 5:21-22, Jesus addresses the issue of anger:

"You have heard that it was said to the people long ago, 'You shall not murder, and anyone who murders will be subject to judgment.' But I tell you that anyone who is angry with a brother or sister will be subject to judgment. Again, anyone who says to a brother or sister, 'Raca,' is answerable to the court. And anyone who says, 'You fool!' will be in danger of the fire of hell."

Here, Jesus equates harboring anger and contempt with the act of murder, highlighting that true love seeks reconciliation and peace, not just the avoidance of physical harm.

Purity of Heart

In Matthew 5:27-28, Jesus extends the command against adultery to include lustful thoughts:

"You have heard that it was said, 'You shall not commit adultery.' But I tell you that anyone who looks at a woman lustfully has already committed adultery with her in his heart."

This teaching emphasizes the importance of purity of heart and thought, reflecting a deeper standard of love and faithfulness that honors others as image-bearers of God.

Love and Generosity

Jesus also teaches about the relationship between love and material possessions. In Matthew 6:19-21, He advises:

"Do not store up for yourselves treasures on earth, where moths and vermin destroy, and where thieves break in and steal. But store up for yourselves treasures in heaven, where moths and vermin do not destroy, and where thieves do not break in and steal. For where your treasure is, there your heart will be also."

This passage calls for a generous and detached attitude towards material wealth, encouraging believers to invest in what is eternal and to prioritize love and generosity over the accumulation of possessions.

The Greatest Commandments

Loving God and Neighbor

In Matthew 22:36-40, Jesus is asked about the greatest commandment in the Law. His response succinctly encapsulates His teachings on love:

"'Teacher, which is the greatest commandment in the Law?' Jesus replied: 'Love the Lord your God with all your heart and with all your soul and with all your mind. This is the first and greatest commandment. And the second is like it: Love your neighbor as yourself. All the Law and the Prophets hang on these two commandments.'"

Jesus identifies love for God and love for neighbor as the two greatest commandments, linking them inseparably. This dual commandment forms the foundation for all ethical and moral behavior, emphasizing that genuine love for God will naturally manifest in love for others.

The Parable of the Good Samaritan

In Luke 10:25-37, Jesus further illustrates the command to love one's neighbor through the Parable of the Good Samaritan. When asked, "And who is my neighbor?" Jesus tells the story of a Samaritan who shows compassion to a beaten and robbed man, unlike the priest and Levite who pass by. The Samaritan's actions exemplify selfless love and compassion, transcending social and ethnic boundaries.

Jesus concludes with a command: "Go and do likewise." This parable underscores that love for neighbor is not limited by proximity or similarity but extends to all, especially those in need.

Love as the Mark of Discipleship

A New Commandment

In John 13:34-35, Jesus gives His disciples a new commandment: "A new command I give you: Love one another. As I have loved you, so you must love one another. By this everyone will know that you are my disciples, if you love one another."

This commandment highlights the centrality of love in the Christian community. The distinguishing mark of Jesus' followers is their love for one another, modeled after the selfless, sacrificial love that Jesus Himself demonstrated.

Abiding in Love

In John 15:9-13, Jesus speaks about the importance of abiding in His love:

"As the Father has loved me, so have I loved you. Now remain in my love. If you keep my commands, you will remain in my love, just as I have kept my Father's commands and remain in His love. I have told you this so that my joy may be in you and that your joy may be complete. My command is this: Love each other as I have loved you. Greater love has no one than this: to lay down one's life for one's friends."

Abiding in Jesus' love involves keeping His commandments and loving others as He has loved us. This abiding relationship is characterized by joy, sacrifice, and mutual love.

### Practical Implications of Jesus' Teachings on Love

### Transformative Love

Jesus' teachings on love call for a transformation of heart and behavior. This love is not merely an emotion but a deliberate choice to seek the well-being of others. It involves forgiveness, compassion, and active efforts to reconcile and heal relationships.

### Community and Service

The love that Jesus teaches fosters a sense of community and mutual support. It calls believers to serve one another, bear each other's burdens, and create a welcoming and inclusive environment. This love extends beyond the church to the broader community, reflecting God's love for all.

### Radical Hospitality

Following Jesus' teachings on love involves practicing radical hospitality—welcoming and caring for strangers, the marginalized, and those different from ourselves. This hospitality reflects the inclusive nature of God's love and breaks down barriers that divide people.

Jesus' teachings on love, particularly in the Sermon on the Mount, provide a radical and transformative vision for how His followers are to live. This love is selfless, inclusive, and deeply rooted in the character of God. It calls for a profound internal transformation that manifests in actions of compassion, justice, and mercy.

As we continue to explore the theology of love, let us be inspired by Jesus' teachings. May we strive to embody this radical love in our daily lives, reflecting the heart of God and living as true disciples of Christ. This love has the power to transform individuals, communities, and the world, embodying the Kingdom of God on earth.

## 3.2.0 THE CROSS AND LOVE
## THE DIVINE NATURE OF LOVE

The cross of Christ stands as the ultimate symbol of sacrificial love, embodying the depth of God's commitment to humanity. Through the crucifixion, Jesus not only atones for the sins of the world but also provides a profound demonstration of selfless love. This chapter delves into the sacrificial love of Christ on the cross, exploring its theological significance and practical implications for believers.

The Sacrificial Love of Christ

John 3:16: The Heart of the Gospel

John 3:16 encapsulates the core of the Christian faith: "For God so loved the world that He gave His one and only Son, that whoever believes in Him shall not perish but have eternal life." This verse highlights the sacrificial nature of God's love, demonstrated through the giving of His Son, Jesus Christ. The cross is the ultimate expression of this divine love, where Jesus willingly lays down His life for the salvation of humanity.

Sacrificial love is characterized by selflessness, a willingness to give up one's own comfort, desires, and even life for the sake of others. Jesus' journey to the cross exemplifies this selfless love. In John 15:13, Jesus states, "Greater love has no one than this: to lay down one's life for one's friends." This declaration underscores the magnitude of His sacrifice and sets the standard for true love.

The Theological Significance of the Cross

The cross is central to the doctrine of atonement, where Jesus takes upon Himself the sins of the world and bears the punishment that humanity deserves. This sacrificial act reconciles humanity to God, restoring the broken relationship caused by sin. In Romans 5:8-10, Paul explains, "But God demonstrates His own love for us in this: While we were still sinners, Christ died for us. Since we have now been justified by His blood, how much more shall we be saved from God's wrath through Him? For if, while we were God's enemies, we were reconciled to Him through the death of His Son, how much more, having been reconciled, shall we be saved through His life!"

Substitutionary Sacrifice

The concept of substitution is integral to understanding the cross. Jesus, the sinless Son of God, takes the place of sinful humanity, bearing the wrath and judgment that we deserve. This substitutionary sacrifice fulfills the demands of justice while demonstrating the boundless mercy of God. In 2 Corinthians 5:21, Paul writes, "God made Him who had no sin to be sin for us so that in Him we might become the righteousness of God."

Victory Over Sin and Death

The cross is also a symbol of victory. Through His death and resurrection, Jesus conquers sin and death, securing eternal life for all who believe in Him. In Colossians 2:13-15, Paul describes this victory: "When you were dead in your sins and in the uncircumcision of your flesh, God made you alive with Christ. He forgave us all our sins, having canceled the charge of our legal indebtedness, which stood against us and condemned us; He has taken it away, nailing it to the cross. And having disarmed the powers and authorities, He made a public spectacle of them, triumphing over them by the cross."

The Cross and the Love Commandment

Jesus' New Commandment

In light of the cross, Jesus gives His disciples a new commandment: "A new command I give you: Love one another. As I have loved you, so you must love one another" (John 13:34). The sacrificial love of Christ on the cross becomes the model for how His followers are to love one another. This love is selfless, sacrificial, and unconditional, reflecting the love of Christ.

Loving Enemies

The cross also challenges believers to extend love even to their enemies. Jesus' prayer for His executioners, "Father, forgive them, for they do not know what they are doing" (Luke 23:34), exemplifies the radical nature of His love. This call to love our enemies and pray for those who persecute us (Matthew 5:44) is rooted in the sacrificial love demonstrated on the cross.

The Practical Implications of the Cross

Living a Life of Sacrifice

The cross calls believers to live lives marked by sacrificial love. This involves putting the needs of others above our own, serving selflessly, and giving generously. In Romans 12:1, Paul urges believers, "Therefore, I urge you, brothers and sisters, in view of God's mercy, to offer your bodies as a living sacrifice, holy and pleasing to God—this is your true and proper worship." Living sacrificially is an act of worship and a reflection of the love of Christ.

Forgiveness and Reconciliation

The cross compels believers to pursue forgiveness and reconciliation in their relationships. Just as Christ forgave us, we are called to forgive others. In Colossians 3:13, Paul writes, "Bear with each other and forgive one another if any of you has a grievance against someone. Forgive as the Lord forgave you." Forgiveness is a powerful expression of sacrificial love, breaking the cycle of bitterness and opening the path to healing and restoration.

Bearing One Another's Burdens

Sacrificial love also involves bearing one another's burdens. In Galatians 6:2, Paul exhorts, "Carry each other's burdens, and in this way you will fulfill the law of Christ." This means supporting and caring for one another in times of need, reflecting the selfless love of Christ.

The Cross and Christian Identity

A New Identity in Christ

The cross transforms our identity, making us new creations in Christ. In Galatians 2:20, Paul declares, "I have been crucified with Christ and I no longer live, but Christ lives in me. The life I now live in the body, I live by faith in the Son of God, who loved me and gave Himself for me." This new identity is rooted in the sacrificial love of Christ and calls us to live out that love in every aspect of our lives.

Participation in Christ's Sufferings

Believers are also called to participate in Christ's sufferings, sharing in His sacrificial love. In Philippians 3:10, Paul expresses his desire "to know Christ—yes, to know the power of His resurrection and participation in His sufferings, becoming like Him in His death." This participation involves embracing the cost of discipleship, enduring hardship for the sake of the Gospel, and living out the sacrificial love of Christ.

The Hope of the Resurrection

The cross is not the end of the story; it is followed by the resurrection, which assures us of the ultimate victory of love over death. The hope of the resurrection empowers believers to live sacrificially, knowing that our labor in love is not in vain. In 1 Corinthians 15:58, Paul encourages, "Therefore, my dear brothers and sisters, stand firm. Let nothing move you. Always give yourselves fully to the work of the Lord, because you know that your labor in the Lord is not in vain."

The Cross and the Mission of the Church

Proclaiming the Gospel of Love

The cross shapes the mission of the Church, calling us to proclaim the Gospel of love to the world. In 1 Corinthians 1:23-24, Paul writes, "but we preach Christ crucified: a stumbling block to Jews and foolishness to Gentiles, but to those whom God has called, both Jews and Greeks, Christ the power of God and the wisdom of God." The message of the cross is central to the Church's mission, offering hope and salvation through the sacrificial love of Christ.

Building a Community of Love

The Church is called to be a community that embodies the sacrificial love of Christ. This involves fostering a culture of selfless service, mutual support, and genuine care for one another. In Acts 2:44-47, the early Church is described as a community that shared everything in common, cared for one another's needs, and lived out the love of Christ in tangible ways.

Extending Love to the World

The sacrificial love of the cross compels the Church to extend love beyond its own community to the world. This involves acts of charity, social justice, and advocacy for the marginalized and oppressed. In Matthew 25:35-40, Jesus teaches that whatever we do for the least of these, we do for Him, highlighting the importance of extending Christ's love to all.

The cross of Christ is the ultimate demonstration of sacrificial love, revealing the depth of God's commitment to humanity and providing the means for our redemption and reconciliation. Through His sacrificial death, Jesus not only atones for our sins but also sets the standard for how we are to love one another.

As we continue to explore the theology of love, let us be deeply moved by the sacrificial love of Christ on the cross. May we embrace this love in our own lives, live out its transformative power, and extend it to others. The cross calls us to a higher standard of love, one that is selfless, sacrificial, and redemptive, embodying the very heart of God.

## 3.2.1 THE TRANSFORMATIVE POWER OF CHRIST'S LOVE FOR HUMANITY

The love of Christ, demonstrated most profoundly through His sacrificial death on the cross, has the power to transform individuals, relationships, and entire communities. This chapter explores the transformative power of Christ's love for humanity, examining its impact on our identity, behavior, relationships, and mission.

The love of Christ fundamentally transforms our identity. When we accept Jesus as our Savior, we are no longer defined by our past sins or failures. Instead, we become new creations in Him. In 2 Corinthians 5:17, Paul declares, "Therefore, if anyone is in Christ, the new creation has come: The old has gone, the new is here!" This new identity is rooted in the love of Christ, which renews and redeems us.

Adoption as Children of God

Through Christ's love, we are adopted into God's family. In Galatians 4:4-7, Paul writes, "But when the set time had fully come, God sent His Son, born of a woman, born under the law, to redeem those under the law, that we might receive adoption to sonship. Because you are His sons, God sent the Spirit of His Son into our hearts, the Spirit who calls out, 'Abba, Father.' So you are no longer a slave, but God's child; and since you are His child, God has made you also an heir." This adoption transforms our relationship with God, allowing us to approach Him with the confidence and intimacy of beloved children.

Freedom from Sin

The transformative power of Christ's love also frees us from the bondage of sin. In Romans 6:6-7, Paul explains, "For we know that our old self was crucified with Him so that the body ruled by sin might be done away with, that we should no longer be slaves to sin—because anyone who has died has been set free from sin." This freedom enables us to live in righteousness, reflecting the character of Christ.

The Impact on Behavior

Living Out the Fruit of the Spirit

The love of Christ empowers us to live out the fruit of the Spirit, as described in Galatians 5:22-23: "But the fruit of the Spirit is love, joy, peace, forbearance, kindness, goodness, faithfulness, gentleness and self-control." These virtues reflect the transformative power of Christ's love, shaping our behavior and interactions with others.

Pursuing Holiness

Christ's love calls us to pursue holiness and live lives that honor God. In 1 Peter 1:15-16, Peter writes, "But just as He who called you is holy, so be holy in all you do; for it is written: 'Be holy because I am holy.'" This pursuit of holiness involves rejecting sinful behaviors and embracing a lifestyle that reflects the purity and righteousness of Christ.

Selfless Service

The love of Christ transforms our attitudes toward service and sacrifice. In Philippians 2:3-8, Paul urges believers to imitate Christ's humility and selflessness: "Do nothing out of selfish ambition or vain conceit. Rather, in humility value others above yourselves, not looking to your own interests but each of you to the interests of the others. In your relationships with one another, have the same mindset as Christ Jesus: Who, being in very nature God, did not consider equality with God something to be used to His own advantage; rather, He made Himself nothing by taking the very nature of a servant, being made in human likeness. And being found in appearance as a man, He humbled Himself by becoming obedient to death— even death on a cross!"

The Impact on Relationships

Forgiveness and Reconciliation

The transformative power of Christ's love enables us to forgive others and seek reconciliation. In Ephesians 4:32, Paul writes, "Be kind and compassionate to one another, forgiving each other, just as in Christ God forgave you." Forgiveness is a central aspect of Christ's love, and as His followers, we are called to extend that same forgiveness to others, fostering healing and restoration in our relationships.

Unity in the Body of Christ

Christ's love also transforms our relationships within the Church, fostering unity and mutual support. In Colossians 3:14-15, Paul exhorts believers, "And over all these virtues put on love, which binds them all together in perfect unity. Let the peace of Christ rule in your hearts, since as members of one body you were called to peace. And be thankful." This unity is a powerful testimony to the world of the transformative power of Christ's love.

Loving Others as Christ Loved Us

Jesus commands His followers to love one another as He has loved them. In John 13:34-35, He says, "A new command I give you: Love one another. As I have loved you, so you must love one another. By this everyone will know that you are my disciples if you love one another." This sacrificial, unconditional love is the hallmark of Christian relationships and reflects the transformative power of Christ's love.

The Impact on Mission

The Great Commission

The love of Christ compels us to share the Gospel with others. In Matthew 28:19-20, Jesus gives the Great Commission: "Therefore go and make disciples of all nations, baptizing them in the name of the Father and of the Son and of the Holy Spirit, and teaching them to obey everything I have commanded you. And surely I am with you always, to the very end of the age." The transformative power of Christ's love drives our mission to spread the good news and make disciples.

Compassion for the Lost

Christ's love fills us with compassion for those who do not yet know Him. In Matthew 9:36, we read, "When He saw the crowds, He had compassion on them, because they were harassed and helpless, like sheep without a shepherd." This compassion motivates us to reach out to the lost, offering them the hope and transformation that comes through Christ.

Acts of Justice and Mercy

The transformative power of Christ's love also calls us to engage in acts of justice and mercy. In Micah 6:8, we are reminded of what God requires: "To act justly and to love mercy and to walk humbly with your God." This involves advocating for the oppressed, caring for the marginalized, and working towards a more just and compassionate society.

The Personal Experience of Christ's Love

Transformative Encounters with Jesus

Throughout the New Testament, we see numerous examples of individuals whose lives were transformed by an encounter with Jesus. The story of Zacchaeus, a tax collector, illustrates this transformation. After meeting Jesus, Zacchaeus declares, "Look, Lord! Here and now I give half of my possessions to the poor, and if I have cheated anybody out of anything, I will pay back four times the amount" (Luke 19:8). Jesus responds, "Today salvation has come to this house, because this man, too, is a son of Abraham" (Luke 19:9). Zacchaeus' encounter with Jesus transforms his heart and behavior, demonstrating the power of Christ's love.

The Transforming Power of the Holy Spirit

The Holy Spirit plays a crucial role in the transformative power of Christ's love. In Romans 5:5, Paul writes, "And hope does not put us to shame, because God's love has been poured out into our hearts through the Holy Spirit, who has been given to us." The Holy Spirit works within us to transform our hearts, enabling us to live out the love of Christ in our daily lives.

The Future Hope of Transformation

The Promise of Glorification

The transformative power of Christ's love extends beyond this life. Believers are promised a future transformation, where we will be glorified and made perfect in Christ. In 1 John 3:2, we read, "Dear friends, now we are children of God, and what we will be has not yet been made known. But we know that when Christ appears, we shall be like Him, for we shall see Him as He is." This future hope encourages us to persevere in our journey of transformation, knowing that God's work in us will be completed.

The New Creation

The ultimate expression of the transformative power of Christ's love will be realized in the new creation. In Revelation 21:4-5, we are given a vision of this future: "He will wipe every tear from their eyes. There will be no more death or mourning or crying or pain, for the old order of things has passed away. He who was seated on the throne said, 'I am making everything new!'" This promise of a new heaven and a new earth where Christ's love reigns supreme fills us with hope and motivates us to live out His transformative love in the present.

The transformative power of Christ's love for humanity is profound and far-reaching. It changes our identity, behavior, relationships, and mission, calling us to live in a way that reflects the sacrificial, unconditional love of Christ. Through His love, we are freed from sin, adopted as children of God, and empowered to live lives of holiness, service, and compassion.

As we continue to explore the theology of love, let us be deeply transformed by the love of Christ. May we embrace His love in our own lives, reflect it in our relationships, and extend it to the world, embodying the transformative power of His love in all that we do. This love has the power to change hearts, communities, and ultimately, the world, bringing about the fullness of God's Kingdom on earth.

## 3.3.0 LOVE IN THE EARLY CHURCH

The early Christian communities, as described in the New Testament, exemplify the practice of love in profound and transformative ways. These communities were characterized by their commitment to mutual support, generosity, and unity, reflecting the teachings and love of Christ. This chapter explores the practice of love in the early Church, with a particular focus on Acts 2:42-47, and examines the implications for contemporary Christian communities.

The Early Christian Community: Acts 2:42-47

A Snapshot of Early Christian Life

Acts 2:42-47 provides a vivid snapshot of the life of the early Christian community:

"They devoted themselves to the apostles' teaching and to fellowship, to the breaking of bread and to prayer. Everyone was filled with awe at the many wonders and signs performed by the apostles. All the believers were together and had everything in common. They sold property and possessions to give to anyone who had need. Every day they continued to meet together in the temple courts. They broke bread in their homes and ate together with glad and sincere hearts, praising God and enjoying the favor of all the people. And the Lord added to their number daily those who were being saved."

This passage highlights several key aspects of the early Christian community, each reflecting the love and unity that characterized their fellowship.

Devotion to Apostolic Teaching and Fellowship

Commitment to Teaching

The early Christians were devoted to the apostles' teachings, which included the teachings of Jesus, interpretations of the Hebrew Scriptures, and the application of these teachings to their lives. This commitment to learning and growing in their faith was foundational to their community life. It fostered a shared understanding of God's love and a unified vision for living out that love.

The Importance of Fellowship

Fellowship, or koinonia, was central to the early Christian experience. This term implies a deep, intimate sharing of life and resources. The believers were not merely acquaintances or attendees at the same gatherings; they were a family united by their faith in Christ. This fellowship was expressed through shared meals, communal worship, and mutual support.

The Breaking of Bread and Prayer

Shared Meals

The breaking of bread likely refers both to the Lord's Supper (Eucharist) and to common meals shared among believers. These meals were significant acts of community and worship, symbolizing the unity and love of the body of Christ. Sharing food fostered a sense of belonging and care, reinforcing the bonds of love within the community.

Prayer

Prayer was another vital practice in the early Church. It connected the believers to God and to each other, fostering spiritual unity and dependence on God's guidance and provision. Corporate prayer times allowed the community to seek God's will together, intercede for one another, and express their collective gratitude and praise.

Radical Generosity and Mutual Aid

Everything in Common

A striking feature of the early Christian community was their radical generosity and willingness to share resources. Acts 2:44-45 describes how "all the believers were together and had everything in common. They sold property and possessions to give to anyone who had need." This practice of communal sharing ensured that no one in the community lacked basic necessities.

Selling Property and Possessions

The early Christians demonstrated sacrificial love by selling property and possessions to meet the needs of others. This radical generosity was a tangible expression of their love for one another and their commitment to the teachings of Jesus. It reflected a deep trust in God's provision and a prioritization of communal well-being over individual wealth.

Daily Worship and Joyful Fellowship

Meeting Together Daily

The early Christians met together daily in the temple courts and in their homes. This regular gathering for worship, teaching, and fellowship created a strong sense of community and continuity. It allowed the believers to encourage one another, grow in their faith, and maintain their collective focus on Christ.

Glad and Sincere Hearts

Their gatherings were characterized by joy and sincerity. Acts 2:46 notes that they "broke bread in their homes and ate together with glad and sincere hearts." This joyful fellowship was a testament to the transformative power of Christ's love and the genuine affection they had for one another.

The Impact on the Broader Community

Praising God and Favor with People

The early Christian community's practice of love and unity had a profound impact on the broader community. Their joyful worship and mutual care led them to "praise God and enjoy the favor of all the people" (Acts 2:47). Their lifestyle was attractive and compelling, drawing others to the faith.

Growth of the Church

As a result of their love and witness, "the Lord added to their number daily those who were being saved" (Acts 2:47). The early Church's authentic love and community life served as a powerful testimony to the truth of the Gospel, leading to the continual growth of the Christian movement.

### Theological Reflections on Love in the Early Church

### Embodied Love

The early Christian community embodied the love of Christ in tangible and practical ways. Their commitment to fellowship, generosity, and worship reflected the teachings of Jesus and demonstrated the power of the Holy Spirit at work among them. This embodied love was not merely an ideal but a lived reality that transformed their lives and relationships.

### Communal Identity

The early Christians understood themselves as a communal entity, bound together by their faith in Christ. This communal identity was rooted in love and expressed through mutual support, shared resources, and collective worship. It provided a stark contrast to the individualism and social stratification of the surrounding culture.

### Witness to the World

The love and unity of the early Christian community served as a powerful witness to the world. Their countercultural practices of generosity, fellowship, and joyful worship attracted others to the faith and demonstrated the transformative power of the Gospel. This witness was not merely through words but through the visible and tangible expression of Christ's love in their communal life.

Practical Implications for Contemporary Christian Communities

Fostering Genuine Fellowship

Contemporary Christian communities can learn from the early Church by fostering genuine fellowship. This involves creating environments where believers can share their lives, support one another, and grow together in their faith. Small groups, communal meals, and regular gatherings for worship and prayer can help cultivate this sense of fellowship.

Practicing Radical Generosity

The early Church's practice of radical generosity challenges contemporary Christians to reconsider their approach to wealth and possessions. Practicing generosity involves more than charitable giving; it requires a willingness to share resources sacrificially and to prioritize the needs of others. This might involve supporting community members in need, funding ministries, or investing in social justice initiatives.

Engaging in Daily Worship and Prayer

Daily worship and prayer were central to the life of the early Church. Incorporating regular rhythms of worship and prayer into our lives helps maintain our focus on God and fosters spiritual unity. This can include personal devotional practices, family worship times, and corporate prayer gatherings.

Building Inclusive Communities

The early Church was marked by its inclusivity and care for all members. Contemporary Christian communities should strive to be inclusive, welcoming people from diverse backgrounds and providing support for the marginalized and vulnerable. This involves creating spaces where everyone feels valued and included, regardless of their social, economic, or cultural status.

Living Out a Compelling Witness

The love and unity of the early Church served as a compelling witness to the world. Contemporary Christians are called to live out their faith in ways that reflect the love of Christ and attract others to the Gospel. This involves living lives of integrity, demonstrating the love of Christ in our interactions, and actively engaging in acts of service and justice.

The practice of love in the early Christian communities, as depicted in Acts 2:42-47, provides a powerful model for contemporary believers. Their commitment to fellowship, generosity, and worship reflected the transformative power of Christ's love and served as a compelling witness to the world.

As we continue to explore the theology of love, let us be inspired by the example of the early Church. May we strive to embody the love of Christ in our own communities, fostering genuine fellowship, practicing radical generosity, engaging in regular worship and prayer, building inclusive communities, and living out a compelling witness to the world. The love that characterized the early Christian communities has the power to transform our lives, our relationships, and our world, reflecting the heart of God and advancing His Kingdom on earth.

## 3.3.1 PAULINE THEOLOGY OF LOVE

The Apostle Paul's writings are foundational to understanding the theology of love in the New Testament. Among his many contributions, 1 Corinthians 13 stands out as a profound exposition on the nature, importance, and characteristics of love. This chapter explores Pauline theology of love, focusing on 1 Corinthians 13, and examines its theological depth and practical implications for the Christian life.

The Context of 1 Corinthians 13

The Corinthian Church

Paul's first letter to the Corinthians addresses various issues within the Christian community in Corinth, including divisions, immorality, and disputes over spiritual gifts. Amidst these issues, Paul interjects his discourse on love in chapter 13, emphasizing its supreme importance and its essential role in the life of the Church.

Spiritual Gifts and Love

1 Corinthians 12 discusses the diversity of spiritual gifts within the body of Christ and their intended purpose for building up the Church. However, Paul concludes chapter 12 by pointing to a "more excellent way" (1 Corinthians 12:31)— the way of love. This sets the stage for his profound exposition of love in the following chapter.

The Supremacy of Love (1 Corinthians 13:1-3)

The Necessity of Love

Paul begins by highlighting the necessity of love in all spiritual activities and expressions:

"If I speak in the tongues of men or of angels, but do not have love, I am only a resounding gong or a clanging cymbal. If I have the gift of prophecy and can fathom all mysteries and all knowledge, and if I have a faith that can move mountains, but do not have love, I am nothing. If I give all I possess to the poor and give over my body to hardship that I may boast, but do not have love, I gain nothing." (1 Corinthians 13:1-3)

In these verses, Paul underscores that without love, even the most impressive spiritual gifts and acts of sacrifice are meaningless. Love is the indispensable element that gives value and purpose to all spiritual endeavors.

The Characteristics of Love (1 Corinthians 13:4-7)

A Detailed Description

Paul then provides a detailed description of the characteristics of love, offering a practical and concrete picture of what true Christian love looks like:

"Love is patient, love is kind. It does not envy, it does not boast, it is not proud. It does not dishonor others, it is not self-seeking, it is not easily angered, it keeps no record of wrongs. Love does not delight in evil but rejoices with the truth. It always protects, always trusts, always hopes, always perseveres." (1 Corinthians 13:4-7)

Positive Attributes

- Patience: Love is enduring and long-suffering, willing to bear with others' faults and shortcomings.

- Kindness: Love is actively compassionate and seeks the welfare of others.

Negative Attributes

- Does not envy: Love is not jealous of others' success or blessings.

- Does not boast: Love does not seek to draw attention to itself or its accomplishments.

- Is not proud: Love is humble and does not inflate its own importance.

- Does not dishonor others: Love respects and honors others, avoiding actions that would bring shame or harm.

- Is not self-seeking: Love prioritizes the needs and interests of others above its own.

- Is not easily angered: Love is slow to take offense and maintains self-control.

- Keeps no record of wrongs: Love forgives and does not hold grudges.

Rejoices with the Truth

- Does not delight in evil but rejoices with the truth: Love finds joy in what is true and righteous, rather than in wrongdoing.

Always

- Always protects: Love safeguards and defends others.

- Always trusts: Love believes the best about others and maintains faith in them.

- Always hopes: Love looks forward with optimism and confidence in God's promises.

- Always perseveres: Love endures through trials and difficulties, remaining steadfast.

The Permanence of Love (1 Corinthians 13:8-13)

The Eternal Nature of Love

Paul contrasts the permanence of love with the temporary nature of spiritual gifts:

"Love never fails. But where there are prophecies, they will cease; where there are tongues, they will be stilled; where there is knowledge, it will pass away. For we know in part and we prophesy in part, but when completeness comes, what is in part disappears." (1 Corinthians 13:8-10)

Spiritual gifts, though important, are temporary and will cease when the fullness of God's kingdom is realized. In contrast, love is eternal and will remain forever.

Maturity and Completeness

Paul uses the analogy of growing from childhood to adulthood to illustrate the process of spiritual maturation:

"When I was a child, I talked like a child, I thought like a child, I reasoned like a child. When I became a man, I put the ways of childhood behind me. For now we see only a reflection as in a mirror; then we shall see face to face. Now I know in part; then I shall know fully, even as I am fully known." (1 Corinthians 13:11-12)

In this present age, our understanding is limited and partial. However, when Christ returns, we will experience the fullness of God's love and know Him completely.

Faith, Hope, and Love

Paul concludes with a powerful affirmation of the enduring virtues of the Christian life:

"And now these three remain: faith, hope, and love. But the greatest of these is love." (1 Corinthians 13:13)

While faith and hope are essential, love is supreme. Love is the greatest virtue because it is the very nature of God and the foundation of all Christian ethics.

Theological Reflections on Pauline Love

Love as the Fulfillment of the Law

Paul consistently teaches that love is the fulfillment of the Law. In Romans 13:8-10, he writes:

"Let no debt remain outstanding, except the continuing debt to love one another, for whoever loves others has fulfilled the law. The commandments, 'You shall not commit adultery,' 'You shall not murder,' 'You shall not steal,' 'You shall not covet,' and whatever other command there may be, are summed up in this one command: 'Love your neighbor as yourself.' Love does no harm to a neighbor. Therefore love is the fulfillment of the law."

Love is the guiding principle that encompasses and fulfills all other commandments, directing believers to act in ways that honor God and respect others.

The Source of Love

Paul emphasizes that love originates from God and is poured into our hearts through the Holy Spirit. In Romans 5:5, he explains:

"And hope does not put us to shame, because God's love has been poured out into our hearts through the Holy Spirit, who has been given to us."

The Holy Spirit enables believers to experience and express God's love, transforming their hearts and lives.

Love and Christian Liberty

In Galatians 5:13-14, Paul addresses the concept of Christian liberty, highlighting that true freedom is expressed through love:

"You, my brothers and sisters, were called to be free. But do not use your freedom to indulge the flesh; rather, serve one another humbly in love. For the entire law is fulfilled in keeping this one command: 'Love your neighbor as yourself.'"

Christian liberty is not an excuse for self-indulgence but an opportunity to serve others in love.

Practical Implications of Pauline Theology of Love

Cultivating Love in Community

Pauline's theology of love calls believers to cultivate love within their communities. This involves fostering environments of mutual respect, support, and encouragement. Churches and Christian groups should prioritize love in their interactions, resolving conflicts with grace and compassion, and seeking to build each other up.

Living Out Love in Action

Love, according to Paul, is not merely an emotion but an active force. Christians are called to demonstrate love through tangible actions, such as helping those in need, forgiving others, and advocating for justice. In 1 John 3:18, the Apostle John echoes this sentiment: "Dear children, let us not love with words or speech but with actions and in truth."

Personal Growth in Love

Individuals are encouraged to grow in their capacity to love by seeking the Holy Spirit's guidance and empowerment. This involves regular prayer, a meditation on Scripture, and a commitment to practicing love in daily life. Believers should also seek accountability and support from their community to help them grow in love.

Love as a Witness

The practice of love serves as a powerful witness to the world. Jesus teaches that love is the distinguishing mark of His disciples: "By this, everyone will know that you are my disciples, if you love one another" (John 13:35). When Christians live out the love described by Paul, it attracts others to the faith and demonstrates the transformative power of the Gospel.

Pauline theology of love, as encapsulated in 1 Corinthians 13, provides a comprehensive and profound understanding of the nature, importance, and characteristics of love. Paul emphasizes that love is the supreme virtue, essential for all spiritual activities, and the fulfillment of the Law.

As we continue to explore the theology of love, let us be inspired by Paul's teachings. May we strive to embody the love described in 1 Corinthians 13, cultivating it within our communities, living it out through our actions, and growing in our capacity to love through the Holy Spirit. The transformative power of this love has the potential to change our lives, our relationships, and our world, reflecting the very heart of God and advancing His Kingdom on earth.

# CHAPTER 04

---

## THEOLOGICAL REFLECTIONS ON LOVE

4.1. Agape: Divine and Selfless Love

The concept of love in Christian theology reaches its highest expression in the term agape. This Greek word, often translated as "divine love" or "selfless love," captures the essence of God's nature and His relationship with humanity. This chapter explores the nature and characteristics of agape love, examining its theological significance and its implications for the Christian life.

Agape love is fundamentally divine in origin. It is the love that God has for humanity and the love that He calls His followers to exhibit. In 1 John 4:8, we read, "Whoever does not love does not know God, because God is love." This statement underscores that agape is not just an attribute of God but the very essence of His being.

Agape love is unconditional and unmerited. Unlike other forms of love that may be based on mutual affection or attraction, agape is given without regard to the worthiness or actions of the recipient. Romans 5:8 illustrates this profound truth: "But God demonstrates His own love for us in this: While we were still sinners, Christ died for us." God's agape love is extended to humanity even in our fallen state, without requiring anything in return.

At the heart of agape love is sacrifice and self-giving. The ultimate demonstration of agape is found in Jesus Christ's sacrificial death on the cross. John 15:13 captures this essence: "Greater love has no one than this: to lay down one's life for one's friends." Agape involves a willingness to give of oneself for the benefit of others, even at great personal cost.

Characteristics of Agape Love

Patient and Kind

Agape love is characterized by patience and kindness. In 1 Corinthians 13:4, Paul describes love: "Love is patient, love is kind." This patience reflects a long-suffering nature that endures through difficulties without becoming resentful. Kindness, on the other hand, involves active goodness and a readiness to help and serve others.

Humble and Unassuming

Agape love is humble and unassuming. It "does not envy, it does not boast, it is not proud" (1 Corinthians 13:4). This humility means that agape does not seek to elevate itself above others but rather esteems others and seeks their good. It avoids jealousy and pride, which can disrupt relationships and community.

Forgiving and Merciful

Forgiveness and mercy are integral to agape love. In Ephesians 4:32, Paul exhorts believers to "be kind and compassionate to one another, forgiving each other, just as in Christ God forgave you." Agape love does not hold grudges or keep a record of wrongs but extends forgiveness and seeks reconciliation.

Rejoices in Truth and Righteousness

Agape love delights in truth and righteousness. It "does not delight in evil but rejoices with the truth" (1 Corinthians 13:6). This characteristic means that agape is aligned with what is right and true, promoting justice and integrity. It opposes falsehood and wrongdoing and celebrates what is good and just.

Protective, Trusting, Hopeful, and Persevering

Agape love is protective, trusting, hopeful, and persevering. Paul continues in 1 Corinthians 13:7: "It always protects, always trusts, always hopes, always perseveres."

These attributes reflect a steadfast commitment to the well-being of others, a belief in their potential, an optimistic outlook on their future, and an unwavering endurance through trials.

Theological Significance of Agape Love

Agape love reflects the very nature of God. As 1 John 4:16 states, "God is love. Whoever lives in love lives in God, and God in them." When we practice agape love, we participate in the divine nature and reflect God's character to the world. This divine love is the foundation of Christian ethics and the guiding principle for all actions and relationships.

Foundation of Christian Ethics

Agape love is the foundation of Christian ethics. Jesus summarized the Law and the Prophets with the commandments to love God and love our neighbor (Matthew 22:37-40). Agape is the principle that undergirds all moral actions and decisions, directing believers to act in ways that honor God and respect others.

Basis for Christian Unity

Agape love is the basis for Christian unity. In John 17:21, Jesus prays for His followers: "that all of them may be one, Father, just as you are in me and I am in you. May they also be in us so that the world may believe that you have sent me." This unity is achieved through the practice of agape love, which binds believers together in mutual affection and commitment.

Implications for the Christian Life

Embracing agape love leads to personal transformation. As believers internalize and practice this divine love, their character and behavior are increasingly conformed to the image of Christ. This transformation involves cultivating the virtues associated with agape, such as patience, kindness, humility, and forgiveness.

Community Building

Agape love is essential for building and sustaining Christian communities. It fosters an environment of mutual support, respect, and care, where individuals are valued and their needs are met. Practicing agape within the community involves acts of service, generosity, and encouragement, contributing to a healthy and vibrant church life.

Social Engagement

Agape love extends beyond the church to society at large. It motivates believers to engage in acts of social justice, mercy, and compassion. This might include advocating for the marginalized, providing for the needy, and working toward systemic changes that reflect the values of the Kingdom of God.

Evangelistic Witness

The practice of agape love serves as a powerful evangelistic witness. In John 13:35, Jesus states, "By this everyone will know that you are my disciples if you love one another." When Christians demonstrate agape love in their relationships and actions, they bear witness to the transformative power of the Gospel and attract others to the faith.

Practical Steps to Cultivate Agape Love

Spiritual Disciplines

Cultivating agape love involves engaging in spiritual disciplines such as prayer, meditation on Scripture, and worship. These practices help believers to deepen their relationship with God and to be filled with His love, enabling them to love others more fully.

Intentional Relationships

Building intentional relationships with others is key to practicing agape love. This involves actively seeking opportunities to serve, support, and encourage others. It requires a commitment to listen, empathize, and walk alongside others in their journeys.

Acts of Service

Practicing agape love through acts of service is a tangible way to express this divine love. This can include volunteering, helping those in need, and participating in community outreach. Serving others selflessly reflects the sacrificial nature of agape love.

Forgiveness and Reconciliation

Agape love calls for forgiveness and reconciliation in relationships. This involves letting go of grudges, extending grace to those who have wronged us, and seeking to mend broken relationships. Practicing forgiveness reflects the merciful nature of agape and promotes healing and unity.

Commitment to Justice

Agape love drives a commitment to justice and righteousness. This involves standing against injustice, advocating for the oppressed, and working towards a fair and equitable society. Engaging in social justice efforts is a way to live out the truth and righteousness that agape rejoices in.

Agape love, as divine and selfless love, is the highest form of love and the very essence of God's nature. It is characterized by patience, kindness, humility, forgiveness, truth, protection, trust, hope, and perseverance. This love reflects God's nature, forms the foundation of Christian ethics, and serves as the basis for Christian unity.

As we continue to explore the theology of love, let us strive to embody agape love in our lives. May we cultivate this divine love through spiritual disciplines, intentional relationships, acts of service, forgiveness, and a commitment to justice. The transformative power of agape love has the potential to change our hearts, build strong communities, and bear witness to the world of the love of God. This love, rooted in the divine and expressed in selfless actions, is the heart of the Christian faith and the key to living a life that honors God and blesses others.

## 4.1.0 THE DISTINCTION BETWEEN AGAPE AND OTHER FORMS OF LOVE

In Christian theology, understanding the various forms of love is crucial for comprehending the full spectrum of human and divine relationships. The New Testament frequently uses the term agape to describe divine, selfless love. However, other Greek words—eros, philia, and storge—also depict different aspects of love. This chapter explores the distinctions between agape and these other forms of love, highlighting their unique characteristics and roles in the Christian life.

Agape: Divine and Selfless Love

Nature and Characteristics

Agape is the highest form of love, characterized by its divine origin and selfless nature. It is unconditional, sacrificial, and unwavering. As discussed in 1 Corinthians 13, agape is patient, kind, humble, forgiving, and rejoices in truth and righteousness. It is the love that God has for humanity and that He calls believers to extend to others.

Biblical Foundation

Agape is central to the New Testament's message of love. John 3:16 encapsulates this divine love: "For God so loved the world that He gave His one and only Son, that whoever believes in Him shall not perish but have eternal life." Similarly, 1 John 4:8 declares, "Whoever does not love does not know God, because God is love." These passages underscore that agape is not just an attribute of God but His very essence.

Expression in Christian Life

In the Christian life, agape is the guiding principle for all actions and relationships. Jesus commands His followers to love one another as He has loved them (John 13:34). This love is to be evident in acts of service, forgiveness, and sacrificial giving. It is the hallmark of true discipleship and the foundation of Christian ethics.

Eros: Romantic and Passionate Love

Nature and Characteristics

Eros refers to romantic, passionate love. It is often associated with physical attraction and desire between partners. While eros can be a powerful and positive force, it is also susceptible to being misdirected or becoming self-centered if not properly guided by agape.

Biblical Context

The term eros does not appear in the New Testament, but the concept of romantic love is present in the Bible, particularly in the Song of Solomon. This poetic book celebrates the beauty and passion of romantic love between a bride and groom, reflecting God's design for marital intimacy. Proverbs 5:18-19 also speaks positively of romantic love within marriage: "May your fountain be blessed, and may you rejoice in the wife of your youth. A loving doe, a graceful deer—may her breasts satisfy you always, may you ever be intoxicated with her love."

Expression in Christian Life

Eros is meant to be experienced within the covenant of marriage, where it can flourish in a context of commitment and mutual respect. It is a gift from God that enhances the marital relationship and contributes to the emotional and physical bond between spouses. However, eros should be guided by agape to ensure it remains selfless and respectful.

Philia: Brotherly and Friendship Love

Nature and Characteristics

Philia refers to affectionate regard and friendship. It is the love that exists between close friends and is characterized by mutual respect, shared interests, and loyalty. Philia is a reciprocal love that involves give-and-take and is based on mutual affection and common values.

Biblical Context

Philia is evident in the New Testament in the context of Christian fellowship and community. In John 15:13-15, Jesus speaks of His disciples as friends: "Greater love has no one than this: to lay down one's life for one's friends. You are my friends if you do what I command. I no longer call you servants, because a servant does not know his master's business. Instead, I have called you friends, for everything that I learned from my Father I have made known to you." This passage highlights the deep, personal connection that philia represents.

Expression in Christian Life

Philia plays a crucial role in the life of the Church. It fosters a sense of community, mutual support, and encouragement among believers. Acts 2:42-47 describes the early Christian community's commitment to fellowship (koinonia), which is deeply rooted in philia. This type of love strengthens the bonds between members of the Church and helps to build a supportive and nurturing environment.

Storge: Familial and Affectionate Love

Nature and Characteristics

Storge refers to natural affection, especially that which exists between family members. It is the love parents have for their children, children for their parents, and siblings for each other. Storge is characterized by its protective, nurturing, and enduring nature.

Biblical Context

While the term storge is not frequently used in the New Testament, the concept is pervasive throughout the Bible. Romans 12:10, which exhorts believers to "be devoted to one another in love," uses the compound word philostorgos, combining philia and storge. This indicates a deep, affectionate love among the family of believers. Additionally, numerous passages emphasize the importance of family relationships and the love that should characterize them, such as Ephesians 6:1-4, which instructs children to honor their parents and parents to nurture their children.

Expression in Christian Life

Storge is essential for healthy family relationships and provides a foundation for emotional and psychological well-being. In the Christian context, this love is extended beyond biological family to the broader family of faith. Believers are called to exhibit storge by caring for one another in practical ways, supporting each other through life's challenges, and creating a sense of belonging and security within the Church.

Interrelation of Agape, Eros, Philia, and Storge

Complementary Loves

While agape, eros, philia, and storge are distinct forms of love, they are not mutually exclusive. In fact, they complement and enhance one another when properly integrated. Agape serves as the guiding principle that elevates and perfects the other forms of love, ensuring they are expressed in ways that honor God and respect others.

Agape Elevating Other Loves

- Agape and Eros: When agape guides eros, romantic love becomes more than just physical attraction; it is transformed into a selfless and committed relationship that reflects God's love. This sanctified eros is patient, kind, and seeks the best for the other person.

- Agape and Philia: When agape infuses philia, friendships become deeper and more meaningful. This divine love adds a dimension of spiritual support and encouragement, fostering genuine Christian fellowship and accountability.

- Agape and Storge: When agape enriches storge, family love transcends mere biological ties. It becomes a reflection of God's nurturing and protective love, creating a strong and stable environment for growth and development.

Holistic Christian Love

In the Christian life, believers are called to practice a holistic love that incorporates agape, eros, philia, and storge. This comprehensive approach to love reflects the fullness of God's character and provides a balanced and healthy expression of love in all relationships.

Practical Applications of Distinguishing Loves

In Marriage

Understanding the distinctions and interrelations between agape, eros, philia, and storge can enhance marital relationships. Couples can strive to cultivate eros within the framework of agape, ensuring that their romantic love is selfless and committed. They can also nurture philia by building a strong friendship and storge by creating a loving and supportive family environment.

In Friendships

In friendships, integrating agape with philia can lead to deeper and more enduring bonds. Friends can practice selfless love by supporting each other in times of need, encouraging spiritual growth, and holding each other accountable to live according to Christian principles.

In Families

Within families, agape can elevate storge, fostering an environment of unconditional love and support. Parents can demonstrate agape by sacrificially caring for their children and teaching them to love others in the same way. Siblings can practice philia and storge by supporting each other and maintaining strong family ties.

In the Church

The Church as a community can embody all forms of love, with agape as the foundation. This holistic love fosters unity, mutual support, and effective witness to the world. Church members can practice philia through fellowship, storge by caring for one another as a family, and agape by serving the broader community selflessly.

Understanding the distinctions between agape, eros, philia, and storge is essential for comprehending the full spectrum of love in Christian theology. While each form of love has its unique characteristics and roles, they are interconnected and enriched by agape—the highest form of divine and selfless love.

As we continue to explore the theology of love, let us strive to practice a holistic love that reflects the fullness of God's character. May we cultivate agape in all our relationships, allowing it to guide and elevate eros, philia, and storge. By doing so, we can experience and express the transformative power of love in our lives, our communities, and the world, reflecting the heart of God and advancing His Kingdom on earth.

## 4.2.0 LOVE AND JUSTICE

In Christian theology, love and justice are not opposing concepts but are deeply intertwined in the character of God. Understanding the interplay between love and justice is essential for comprehending how God relates to humanity and how believers are called to live. This chapter explores the relationship between love and justice in the character of God, examining biblical foundations and theological implications.

The Character of God: Love and Justice

God as Love

The Bible unequivocally declares that God is love. 1 John 4:8 states, "Whoever does not love does not know God, because God is love." This affirmation highlights that love is not merely an attribute of God but the very essence of His being. God's actions and relationships are fundamentally rooted in love, encompassing compassion, mercy, and grace.

God as Just

Equally, the Bible affirms that God is just. Psalm 89:14 proclaims, "Righteousness and justice are the foundation of your throne; love and faithfulness go before you." Justice, in this context, refers to God's commitment to what is right and fair, ensuring that good is rewarded, and evil is punished. God's justice reflects His holiness and moral perfection.

The Interplay Between Love and Justice

Love and justice are not contradictory but complementary aspects of God's character. God's justice ensures that His love is not permissive or indulgent but righteous and redemptive. Conversely, God's love ensures that His justice is not harsh or unyielding but compassionate and restorative. Together, love and justice form a harmonious whole, revealing a God who is both infinitely loving and perfectly just.

Biblical Foundations of Love and Justice

The Old Testament Perspective

In the Old Testament, God's love and justice are often depicted in His covenantal relationship with Israel. God's covenant with Israel is characterized by His steadfast love (hesed) and His commitment to justice.

Micah 6:8

One of the clearest expressions of the interplay between love and justice is found in Micah 6:8: "He has shown you, O mortal, what is good. And what does the Lord require of you? To act justly and to love mercy and to walk humbly with your God." This verse encapsulates the essential requirements of a life pleasing to God: justice, mercy, and humility.

Isaiah's Prophecies

The book of Isaiah frequently addresses the themes of love and justice. In Isaiah 1:17, God calls His people to "Learn to do right; seek justice. Defend the oppressed. Take up the cause of the fatherless; plead the case of the widow." Here, justice is portrayed as an active pursuit, inseparable from acts of love and mercy.

The New Testament Perspective

The New Testament continues to emphasize the unity of love and justice, particularly through the teachings and actions of Jesus Christ.

The Teachings of Jesus

Jesus' teachings consistently reflect the balance of love and justice. In the Sermon on the Mount, Jesus calls His followers to a higher standard of righteousness that goes beyond mere legalistic adherence to the law. In Matthew 5:6, He states, "Blessed are those who hunger and thirst for righteousness, for they will be filled." This righteousness encompasses both personal piety and social justice.

The Parable of the Good Samaritan

The Parable of the Good Samaritan (Luke 10:25-37) illustrates the interplay between love and justice. In this parable, a Samaritan helps a wounded man, showing compassion and providing for his needs. Jesus concludes by instructing His listeners to "go and do likewise," emphasizing that true love involves acts of justice and mercy.

Paul's Theology

The Apostle Paul also addresses the relationship between love and justice. In Romans 12:9-21, Paul exhorts believers to "hate what is evil; cling to what is good" and to "practice hospitality." He emphasizes that love must be sincere and that believers should "overcome evil with good." This passage highlights that love and justice are interdependent, with love guiding the pursuit of justice.

The Cross as the Ultimate Expression of Love and Justice

The Atonement

The cross of Christ is the ultimate demonstration of the interplay between love and justice. In the atonement, God's love and justice are perfectly reconciled. Through Jesus' sacrificial death, God addresses the problem of sin with both justice and mercy.

Romans 3:25-26

Paul explains this profound truth in Romans 3:25-26: "God presented Christ as a sacrifice of atonement, through the shedding of His blood—to be received by faith. He did this to demonstrate His righteousness because in His forbearance He had left the sins committed beforehand unpunished—He did it to demonstrate His righteousness at the present time, so as to be just and the one who justifies those who have faith in Jesus." Here, God's justice is upheld as sin is punished, and His love is manifested as sinners are justified and reconciled to Him.

The Transformative Power of the Cross

The cross not only reconciles love and justice but also transforms believers. Through the cross, believers are called to a new way of life, marked by love and a commitment to justice. This transformation is empowered by the Holy Spirit, enabling believers to live out the values of the Kingdom of God.

Theological Implications of Love and Justice

Divine Love as the Foundation of Justice

In Christian theology, divine love is the foundation of justice. God's justice is not arbitrary but flows from His loving nature. This means that God's judgments are always fair, righteous, and aimed at the ultimate good of His creation. Understanding justice as rooted in love helps believers to see justice not merely as retribution but as restoration and reconciliation.

Human Responsibility

Believers are called to reflect God's character by embodying both love and justice in their lives. This involves advocating for the oppressed, caring for the vulnerable, and working toward a just society. It also requires personal integrity, honesty, and a commitment to righteousness in all aspects of life.

Social Justice

The interplay between love and justice has significant implications for social justice. Christians are called to engage in social justice efforts, motivated by love for God and neighbor. This includes addressing systemic injustices, standing against oppression, and promoting equity and fairness. Social justice is an expression of the Kingdom of God, where love and justice reign.

Practical Applications of Love and Justice

Advocacy and Action

Believers are called to advocate for justice and take action to address injustices in their communities and the world. This can involve participating in or supporting organizations that work for social justice, engaging in advocacy efforts, and being a voice for the marginalized and oppressed.

Compassionate Service

Compassionate service is a practical expression of love and justice. This involves meeting the immediate needs of those who are suffering, such as providing food, shelter, and medical care. It also includes longer-term efforts to address the root causes of poverty and inequality.

Peacemaking and Reconciliation

Peacemaking and reconciliation are essential aspects of love and justice. Believers are called to be peacemakers, working to resolve conflicts and promote harmony. This involves seeking reconciliation in personal relationships, as well as contributing to efforts that promote peace and justice in broader social and political contexts.

Personal Integrity and Ethical Living

Living with personal integrity and ethical behavior is a reflection of love and justice. This includes being honest, fair, and righteous in all dealings, whether in personal relationships, business, or public life. It also involves holding oneself accountable to God's standards of justice and righteousness.

Community Building

Building strong, loving, and just communities is a practical way to live out the interplay between love and justice. This involves fostering inclusive, supportive, and caring environments where everyone is valued and treated with dignity. It includes creating spaces where people can grow, thrive, and contribute to the common good.

The interplay between love and justice is a central theme in Christian theology, reflecting the very character of God. Understanding this relationship helps believers see that true love includes a commitment to justice and that genuine justice is rooted in love. Together, love and justice form the foundation for righteous living and the pursuit of the Kingdom of God.

As we continue to explore the theology of love, let us strive to embody both love and justice in our lives. May we be inspired by the example of Jesus, who perfectly demonstrated this interplay on the cross, and may we seek to reflect His character in our actions and relationships. By doing so, we can contribute to a world where love and justice prevail, advancing the Kingdom of God on earth and bringing glory to His name.

## 4.2.1 THE IMPLICATIONS OF A THEOLOGY OF LOVE FOR SOCIAL JUSTICE

A theology of love that encompasses divine, selfless agape love, as well as the interplay between love and justice, has profound implications for social justice. This chapter explores these implications, examining how a robust understanding of Christian love compels believers to engage in social justice efforts, advocate for the marginalized, and work towards a more equitable and compassionate society.

The Foundation of Social Justice in Christian Love

Divine Mandate for Justice

The Bible consistently calls for justice, rooted in God's character of love. As reflected in Micah 6:8, believers are commanded to "act justly and to love mercy and to walk humbly with your God." This divine mandate underpins the Christian imperative to engage in social justice, reflecting God's love and righteousness in societal structures and relationships.

Agape Love as Motivation

Agape love—selfless, unconditional love—motivates believers to pursue social justice. This form of love seeks the well-being of others, particularly the vulnerable and oppressed. In 1 John 3:17-18, the apostle John challenges believers: "If anyone has material possessions and sees a brother or sister in need but has no pity on them, how can the love of God be in that person? Dear children, let us not love with words or speech but with actions and in truth." Agape love moves beyond sentiment to tangible actions that address injustice and promote equity.

Theological Basis for Social Justice

Imago Dei: The Image of God

The doctrine of imago Dei—the belief that all humans are created in the image of God (Genesis 1:27)—provides a theological basis for social justice. This doctrine affirms the inherent dignity, worth, and equality of every person. Recognizing the image of God in others compels believers to advocate for the rights and well-being of all people, particularly those who are marginalized or oppressed.

The Kingdom of God

The concept of the Kingdom of God, central to Jesus' teaching, encompasses both spiritual and social dimensions. Jesus' ministry demonstrated the inbreaking of God's Kingdom, characterized by justice, peace, and love. In Luke 4:18-19, Jesus declares His mission: "The Spirit of the Lord is on me because he has anointed me to proclaim good news to the poor. He has sent me to proclaim freedom for the prisoners and recovery of sight for the blind, to set the oppressed free, to proclaim the year of the Lord's favor." This mission underscores the commitment to social justice as a reflection of the Kingdom of God.

The Great Commandments

The Great Commandments—to love God and love neighbor (Matthew 22:37-40)—form the ethical foundation for social justice. Loving one's neighbor involves seeking their well-being and advocating for their rights. This love extends beyond personal relationships to address systemic issues that affect communities and societies.

Practical Implications for Social Justice

Advocacy and Activism

Speaking Out Against Injustice

Believers are called to be advocates for justice, speaking out against injustice and working to change unjust systems. This involves raising awareness about issues such as poverty, racism, human trafficking, and environmental degradation. Advocacy can take various forms, including public speaking, writing, campaigning, and lobbying for policy changes.

Supporting Social Justice Movements

Christians can support social justice movements that align with biblical principles of justice and equity. This support can include participating in peaceful protests, joining organizations that work for social change, and collaborating with others who are committed to justice.

Compassionate Service

Meeting Immediate Needs

A theology of love compels believers to meet the immediate needs of those who are suffering. This includes providing food, shelter, medical care, and other essential services to individuals and communities in need. Acts of compassionate service reflect the love of Christ and provide practical assistance to those facing hardship.

### Long-Term Development

In addition to meeting immediate needs, Christians are called to engage in long-term development efforts that address the root causes of poverty and injustice. This can involve initiatives such as education, economic empowerment, healthcare, and community development. These efforts aim to create sustainable change and improve the quality of life for marginalized communities.

### Restorative Justice

### Healing and Reconciliation

Restorative justice focuses on healing and reconciliation rather than retribution. It seeks to repair the harm caused by wrongdoing and restore relationships between victims, offenders, and the community. This approach aligns with the biblical principles of forgiveness, mercy, and redemption. Believers can promote restorative justice by supporting programs that facilitate reconciliation and rehabilitation.

### Advocating for Fairness in the Legal System

Christians are called to advocate for fairness and equity in the legal system. This includes addressing issues such as racial disparities in sentencing, the treatment of prisoners, and access to legal representation. By working to ensure that the legal system reflects the principles of justice and compassion, believers can help create a more just society.

Economic Justice

Fair Wages and Employment Practices

A theology of love calls for fair wages and equitable employment practices. This involves advocating for living wages, safe working conditions, and the rights of workers. Christians can support policies and practices that promote economic justice and dignity for all workers.

Addressing Economic Inequality

Believers are called to address economic inequality by supporting initiatives that promote economic empowerment and reduce poverty. This can include programs that provide education, job training, and access to financial resources for marginalized communities. Economic justice efforts reflect the biblical call to care for the poor and vulnerable.

Environmental Justice

Caring for Creation

A theology of love includes a commitment to environmental justice, recognizing that the well-being of creation is intrinsically linked to human well-being. Christians are called to steward the earth responsibly and advocate for policies that protect the environment. This involves addressing issues such as climate change, pollution, and deforestation.

Promoting Sustainable Practices

Believers can promote sustainable practices that protect the environment and support the well-being of future generations. This can include initiatives such as renewable energy, sustainable agriculture, and conservation efforts. By caring for creation, Christians reflect God's love for the world and contribute to a more just and sustainable future.

Building Inclusive and Equitable Communities

Embracing Diversity

A theology of love embraces diversity and promotes inclusivity. Christians are called to welcome and value people of all backgrounds, recognizing the image of God in each person. This involves creating inclusive communities where everyone feels valued and respected.

Promoting Equity

Believers are called to promote equity by addressing disparities and working towards equal opportunities for all. This involves advocating for policies and practices that remove barriers and create a level playing field. By promoting equity, Christians contribute to a more just and inclusive society.

Challenges and Opportunities

Overcoming Resistance

Engaging in social justice can encounter resistance from those who benefit from the status quo or who misunderstand the biblical call to justice. Believers must be prepared to face opposition and remain committed to the principles of love and justice. This involves educating others about the biblical basis for social justice and working to build consensus and support.

Collaborating with Others

Christians can amplify their impact by collaborating with others who are committed to social justice, including non-religious organizations and individuals from different faith traditions. By working together, believers can build coalitions and leverage resources to address complex social issues more effectively.

Sustaining Efforts

Social justice work can be challenging and require long-term commitment. Believers must be prepared to persevere and sustain their efforts over time. This involves nurturing a deep spiritual foundation, seeking God's guidance and strength, and building supportive communities that encourage and sustain one another in the pursuit of justice.

A theology of love has profound implications for social justice, compelling believers to engage in advocacy, compassionate service, restorative justice, economic justice, environmental justice, and the promotion of inclusive and equitable communities. By embodying the love and justice of God, Christians can contribute to a more just and compassionate world, reflecting the values of the Kingdom of God.

As we continue to explore the theology of love, let us be inspired to act justly, love mercy, and walk humbly with our God. May we strive to live out the principles of agape love in all areas of our lives, advocating for justice and working towards a more equitable and compassionate society. By doing so, we can bear witness to the transformative power of God's love and advance His Kingdom on earth.

## 4.3.0 LOVE AND HOLINESS

In Christian theology, love and holiness are deeply intertwined. Holiness is often understood as moral purity and separation from sin, while love is seen as selfless and sacrificial. This chapter explores the relationship between love and holiness in the Christian life, examining how these two fundamental aspects of God's character are reflected in believers and how they shape our spiritual journey.

Holiness is a defining attribute of God. It signifies His moral perfection, purity, and complete separation from sin.

Isaiah 6:3 emphasizes this attribute with the seraphim's declaration: "Holy, holy, holy is the Lord Almighty; the whole earth is full of His glory." God's holiness sets Him apart from all creation and underscores His absolute moral integrity.

Holiness in Believers

Believers are called to reflect God's holiness in their lives. 1 Peter 1:15-16 commands, "But just as He who called you is holy, so be holy in all you do; for it is written: 'Be holy, because I am holy.'" This call to holiness involves living a life that is set apart for God, characterized by moral purity and obedience to His will.

The Nature of Love

Agape Love

As discussed in previous chapters, agape love is divine and selfless, characterized by its unconditional, sacrificial nature. It is the highest form of love, reflecting God's own love for humanity. 1 John 4:8 states, "Whoever does not love does not know God, because God is love." This emphasizes that love is not merely an action but a reflection of God's very essence.

Love in Action

Christian love, as exemplified by Jesus, involves tangible actions that seek the well-being of others. John 13:34-35 highlights this: "A new command I give you: Love one another. As I have loved you, so you must love one another. By this everyone will know that you are my disciples if you love one another." This love is active, manifesting in service, compassion, and sacrifice.

The Interplay Between Love and Holiness

Holiness Expressed Through Love

Holiness and love are not separate or competing attributes but are deeply interconnected. True holiness is expressed through love. 1 John 4:12 states, "No one has ever seen God; but if we love one another, God lives in us and His love is made complete in us." Living a holy life means embodying agape love, which reflects God's nature and His love for us.

Love as the Fulfillment of Holiness

Love fulfills the demands of holiness. Romans 13:10 asserts, "Love does no harm to a neighbor. Therefore love is the fulfillment of the law." The moral and ethical standards of holiness are encapsulated in the command to love. By loving others, believers naturally fulfill God's holy law.

Sanctification Through Love

Sanctification, the process of becoming more like Christ, involves growing in both holiness and love. Ephesians 5:1-2 exhorts, "Follow God's example, therefore, as dearly loved children and walk in the way of love, just as Christ loved us and gave Himself up for us as a fragrant offering and sacrifice to God." Walking in love is integral to the sanctification process, as it aligns believers' lives with the character of Christ.

Biblical Examples of Love and Holiness

Jesus as the Perfect Example

Jesus Christ is the perfect example of the integration of love and holiness. His life, ministry, and sacrificial death exemplify the highest standards of both attributes. In John 17:19, Jesus prays, "For them I sanctify myself, that they too may be truly sanctified." Jesus' holiness was demonstrated through His unwavering obedience to the Father and His selfless love for humanity.

The Early Church

The early Church provides practical examples of love and holiness in action. Acts 2:42-47 describes the believers' commitment to fellowship, sharing possessions, and caring for those in need. This community life was a tangible expression of both their holiness, as they lived set apart for God, and their love, as they cared for one another.

Practical Implications for the Christian Life

Personal Holiness

Believers are called to pursue personal holiness by aligning their lives with God's will and reflecting His character. This involves regular self-examination, repentance, and growth in virtue. Personal holiness is not an end in itself but a means to love others more fully and effectively.

Cultivating Love

Cultivating agape love requires intentionality and effort. Believers can develop this love through spiritual disciplines such as prayer, meditation on Scripture, and acts of service. By seeking to love others selflessly, believers grow in holiness and reflect God's love to the world.

Community Life

The interplay between love and holiness has significant implications for community life within the Church. Believers are called to create communities characterized by mutual support, accountability, and compassion. This involves fostering an environment where holiness is pursued collectively and love is practiced consistently.

Ethical Behavior

Living out the relationship between love and holiness involves ethical behavior in all areas of life. This includes honesty, integrity, justice, and respect for others. By living ethically, believers demonstrate their commitment to both God's holiness and His command to love.

Mission and Evangelism

The relationship between love and holiness also shapes the Church's mission and evangelism efforts. By embodying both attributes, believers present a compelling witness to the world. John 13:35 emphasizes the evangelistic power of love: "By this, everyone will know that you are my disciples, if you love one another." Holiness and love together draw others to Christ and demonstrate the transformative power of the Gospel.

Challenges in Integrating Love and Holiness

Legalism and License

A key challenge in integrating love and holiness is avoiding the extremes of legalism and license. Legalism emphasizes strict adherence to rules at the expense of love, leading to judgmentalism and hypocrisy. License, on the other hand, emphasizes freedom at the expense of holiness, leading to moral laxity and compromise. True Christian living requires balancing love and holiness, avoiding these extremes.

Cultural Pressures

Cultural pressures can also challenge believers in integrating love and holiness. Secular society often promotes values that conflict with biblical standards of holiness and love. Believers must navigate these pressures with discernment, holding fast to God's truth while expressing His love in a contextually relevant way.

Strategies for Cultivating Love and Holiness

Spiritual Disciplines

Engaging in spiritual disciplines such as prayer, fasting, and studying Scripture helps believers grow in both love and holiness. These practices draw believers closer to God, transforming their hearts and minds to reflect His character.

Accountability and Community

Being part of a supportive Christian community provides accountability and encouragement in the pursuit of love and holiness. Small groups, discipleship relationships, and mentoring can help believers stay focused on their spiritual growth and provide practical support for living out their faith.

Service and Mission

Serving others and participating in mission work are practical ways to cultivate love and holiness. Acts of service reflect God's love and help believers grow in humility, compassion, and selflessness. Mission work expands believers' perspectives, challenging them to live out their faith in diverse and often difficult contexts.

Continuous Learning

Believers should commit to continuous learning and growth in their understanding of love and holiness. This can involve reading theological works, attending seminars and conferences, and engaging in discussions with other believers. Continuous learning helps believers deepen their faith and apply it more effectively in their daily lives.

The relationship between love and holiness is integral to the Christian life. These attributes, deeply rooted in the character of God, are not mutually exclusive but are meant to be integrated and expressed together. True holiness is manifested through love, and genuine love fulfills the demands of holiness.

As we continue to explore the theology of love, let us strive to embody both love and holiness in our lives. May we pursue personal holiness through a commitment to God's will and cultivate agape love through selfless service and compassion. By doing so, we reflect God's character to the world and live out the transformative power of the Gospel, drawing others to Christ and advancing His Kingdom on earth.

## 4.3.1 SANCTIFICATION AS A JOURNEY OF GROWING IN LOVE

Sanctification, the process of becoming more like Christ, is fundamentally a journey of growing in love. This chapter explores the relationship between sanctification and love, highlighting how love is both the goal and the means of spiritual growth. We will examine biblical foundations, theological insights, and practical steps for believers to cultivate love as they progress on their journey of sanctification.

The Nature of Sanctification

Biblical Foundation

Sanctification is a key theme in the New Testament, emphasizing the transformation of believers into the image of Christ. 1 Thessalonians 4:3 states, "It is God's will that you should be sanctified." This process involves a continuous journey of spiritual growth, characterized by increasing holiness and alignment with God's will.

The Role of the Holy Spirit

The Holy Spirit plays a central role in sanctification, empowering believers to grow in love and holiness. Galatians 5:22-23 lists the fruit of the Spirit, beginning with love: "But the fruit of the Spirit is love, joy, peace, forbearance, kindness, goodness, faithfulness, gentleness and self-control." The Spirit's work in believers' lives produces these qualities, with love being foundational.

Love as the Goal of Sanctification

The Greatest Commandments

Jesus identifies love as the greatest commandment and the essence of the Law. In Matthew 22:37-40, He states, "'Love the Lord your God with all your heart and with all your soul and with all your mind.' This is the first and greatest commandment. And the second is like it: 'Love your neighbor as yourself.' All the Law and the Prophets hang on these two commandments." Sanctification involves growing in our love for God and others, and aligning our lives with these commandments.

Conformity to Christ's Image

Sanctification aims to conform believers to the image of Christ, who perfectly embodies love. Romans 8:29 explains, "For those God foreknew He also predestined to be conformed to the image of His Son." Jesus' life and ministry exemplify selfless, sacrificial love, and sanctification involves becoming more like Him in our thoughts, actions, and relationships.

Love as the Means of Sanctification

The Transformative Power of Love

Love is not only the goal of sanctification but also the means by which believers are transformed. 1 John 4:16-17 emphasizes the transformative power of love: "God is love. Whoever lives in love lives in God, and God in them. This is how love is made complete among us so that we will have confidence on the day of judgment: In this world, we are like Jesus." Living in love transforms believers into the likeness of Christ, who is love incarnate.

Obedience Motivated by Love

Obedience to God's commands is a crucial aspect of sanctification, and true obedience is motivated by love. In John 14:15, Jesus states, "If you love me, keep my commands." Love for God inspires believers to follow His commandments, and this obedience leads to greater holiness and spiritual growth.

Practical Steps for Growing in Love

Cultivating a Relationship with God

Growing in love begins with cultivating a deep, personal relationship with God. This involves regular practices of prayer, worship, and meditation on Scripture. Spending time in God's presence and immersing ourselves in His Word helps us to understand His love more fully and to reflect that love in our lives.

Practicing the Fruit of the Spirit

The fruit of the Spirit, beginning with love, provides a framework for growing in love. Believers can intentionally cultivate these qualities through daily practices and choices. For example, practicing patience, kindness, and forgiveness in our interactions with others helps to nurture a loving character.

Engaging in Acts of Service

Acts of service are practical expressions of love and a means of growing in love. Serving others, whether through volunteer work, helping a neighbor, or supporting a charitable cause, reflects the selfless love of Christ and fosters spiritual growth. In Galatians 5:13, Paul exhorts, "Serve one another humbly in love."

Building Community and Relationships

Community and relationships are essential contexts for growing in love. Believers are called to engage in authentic, supportive relationships within the Church and beyond. This involves building genuine connections, offering and receiving support, and practicing love in tangible ways. Hebrews 10:24-25 encourages believers to "spur one another on toward love and good deeds, not giving up meeting together, as some are in the habit of doing, but encouraging one another."

Embracing Forgiveness and Reconciliation

Forgiveness and reconciliation are vital aspects of growing in love. Colossians 3:13 instructs, "Bear with each other and forgive one another if any of you has a grievance against someone. Forgive as the Lord forgave you."

Embracing forgiveness and seeking reconciliation reflect God's love and promote healing and unity in relationships.

Seeking the Guidance of the Holy Spirit

The Holy Spirit is the source of love and the guide in our journey of sanctification. Believers are encouraged to seek the Spirit's guidance through prayer and attentiveness to His leading. Romans 5:5 reminds us, "God's love has been poured out into our hearts through the Holy Spirit, who has been given to us." By relying on the Spirit, believers can grow in love and holiness.

Challenges in the Journey of Growing in Love

Overcoming Self-Centeredness

One of the primary challenges in growing in love is overcoming self-centeredness. Our natural inclination is often toward self-interest and self-preservation. Sanctification involves dying to self and learning to prioritize the needs and well-being of others. Philippians 2:3-4 advises, "Do nothing out of selfish ambition or vain conceit. Rather, in humility value others above yourselves, not looking to your own interests but each of you to the interests of the others."

Navigating Difficult Relationships

Difficult relationships can also challenge our ability to grow in love. Loving others who are challenging or who have hurt us requires grace, patience, and a reliance on God's strength. Romans 12:18 encourages, "If it is possible, as far as it depends on you, live at peace with everyone." Seeking God's help in navigating difficult relationships is crucial for growing in love.

Persevering Through Trials

Trials and hardships can test our love and commitment to the sanctification journey. James 1:2-4 offers encouragement, "Consider it pure joy, my brothers and sisters, whenever you face trials of many kinds, because you know that the testing of your faith produces perseverance. Let perseverance finish its work so that you may be mature and complete, not lacking anything." Persevering through trials with a focus on love leads to greater spiritual maturity.

The Outcome of Growing in Love

Maturity in Christ

The outcome of growing in love is maturity in Christ. Ephesians 4:15-16 describes this growth: "Instead, speaking the truth in love, we will grow to become in every respect the mature body of Him who is the head, that is, Christ. From Him, the whole body joined and held together by every supporting ligament, grows and builds itself up in love, as each part does its work." As believers grow in love, they mature in their faith and contribute to the growth of the Church.

Effective Witness

Growing in love enhances believers' witness to the world. Jesus emphasizes this in John 13:35: "By this, everyone will know that you are my disciples if you love one another." A life characterized by agape love is a powerful testimony to the transformative power of the Gospel and attracts others to Christ.

Deeper Relationship with God

As believers grow in love, they experience a deeper relationship with God. Love draws us closer to Him and aligns our hearts with His. 1 John 4:16 assures, "God is love. Whoever lives in love lives in God, and God in them." This deep, abiding relationship with God is the ultimate goal of sanctification.

Sanctification is a journey of growing in love, with agape love as both the goal and the means of spiritual growth. As believers cultivate a deep relationship with God, practice the fruit of the Spirit, engage in acts of service, build community, embrace forgiveness, and seek the guidance of the Holy Spirit, they grow in love and reflect the character of Christ.

While challenges such as self-centeredness, difficult relationships, and trials may arise, perseverance and reliance on God's strength enable believers to continue their journey of sanctification. The outcome of this journey is maturity in

Christ, an effective witness to the world, and a deeper relationship with God.

As we continue to explore the theology of love, let us be committed to growing in love through the process of sanctification. By doing so, we can reflect God's love to the world, contribute to the building up of the Church, and experience the fullness of life in Christ.

# CHAPTER 05

---

## PRACTICAL APPLICATIONS OF LOVE

### 5.1. Love in the Family

Love in the family is a cornerstone of Christian living, reflecting the divine love of God in our most intimate relationships. The Bible provides profound guidance on how love should manifest in marriage and parenting. This chapter explores the biblical foundations for love in the family, examining the principles and practices that nurture healthy, loving relationships within the home.

Love in Marriage

Biblical Foundations

The Covenant of Marriage

Marriage is a sacred covenant designed by God to reflect His relationship with His people. In Genesis 2:24, we read, "That is why a man leaves his father and mother and is united to his wife, and they become one flesh." This union signifies a lifelong commitment and intimate partnership between husband and wife.

Christ and the Church

The Apostle Paul draws a parallel between the marital relationship and Christ's relationship with the Church. In Ephesians 5:25-33, Paul exhorts husbands to "love your wives, just as Christ loved the church and gave Himself up for her." This sacrificial love is the model for marital love, characterized by selflessness, service, and devotion.

Principles for Loving Marriages

Mutual Submission

Ephesians 5:21 instructs, "Submit to one another out of reverence for Christ." Mutual submission involves honoring and valuing each other's needs, preferences, and well-being. It requires humility, respect, and a willingness to serve one another in love.

Sacrificial Love

Husbands are called to love their wives sacrificially, as Christ loved the Church. This involves prioritizing the wife's needs, protecting her, and nurturing her spiritual and emotional growth. Sacrificial love is not about dominance but about laying down one's life for the other's benefit.

Respect and Honor

Wives are called to respect and honor their husbands. In Ephesians 5:33, Paul writes, "The wife must respect her husband." Respect involves recognizing the husband's role and affirming his leadership, while honor entails valuing his contributions and expressing appreciation.

Companionship and Intimacy

Marriage is designed for companionship and intimacy. Ecclesiastes 4:9-12 highlights the value of partnership: "Two are better than one because they have a good return for their labor: If either of them falls down, one can help the other up." Companionship involves sharing life together, building emotional and physical intimacy, and providing mutual support.

Love in Parenting

Biblical Foundations

The Role of Parents

Parents are entrusted with the responsibility of raising their children in the knowledge and fear of the Lord. Deuteronomy 6:6-7 emphasizes the importance of teaching children God's commands: "These commandments that I give you today are to be on your hearts. Impress them on your children. Talk about them when you sit at home and when you walk along the road, when you lie down and when you get up."

Children as Gifts from God

Psalm 127:3-5 declares, "Children are a heritage from the Lord, offspring a reward from Him. Like arrows in the hands of a warrior are children born in one's youth. Blessed is the man whose quiver is full of them." Recognizing children as gifts from God encourages parents to value and nurture them with love and care.

Principles for Loving Parenting

Nurturing and Training

Parents are called to nurture and train their children in the ways of the Lord. Ephesians 6:4 instructs, "Fathers, do not exasperate your children; instead, bring them up in the training and instruction of the Lord." Nurturing involves providing emotional support, while training encompasses teaching discipline and guiding moral and spiritual development.

Discipline and Correction

Loving discipline is essential for a child's growth and character formation. Proverbs 13:24 states, "Whoever spares the rod hates their children, but the one who loves their children is careful to discipline them." Discipline should be administered with love, aiming to correct and instruct rather than to punish harshly.

Unconditional Love and Acceptance

Children need to experience unconditional love and acceptance from their parents. This means loving them regardless of their behavior or achievements. 1 Corinthians

13:7 captures this essence: "Love always protects, always trusts, always hopes, always perseveres." Unconditional love builds a child's self-esteem and sense of security.

### Modeling Godly Character

Parents are called to model godly character in their own lives. Children learn by observing their parents' actions and attitudes. Deuteronomy 6:6-7 emphasizes the importance of parents embodying the values they teach: "These commandments that I give you today are to be on your hearts. Impress them on your children."

### Building Strong Family Bonds

### Quality Time

Spending quality time together strengthens family bonds. This involves engaging in activities that foster connection, such as shared meals, family devotions, and recreational activities. Quality time allows family members to build trust, communicate openly, and create lasting memories.

### Open Communication

Healthy families practice open and honest communication. Ephesians 4:15 encourages speaking the truth in love. Parents should create an environment where children feel safe to express their thoughts and feelings. Open communication fosters understanding and resolves conflicts constructively.

Shared Faith and Worship

Sharing faith and worship as a family nurtures spiritual growth and unity. Joshua 24:15 declares, "But as for me and my household, we will serve the Lord." Family devotions, prayer, and attending church together reinforce a shared commitment to God and His purposes.

Encouragement and Affirmation

Encouragement and affirmation are vital for building a child's confidence and sense of worth. Proverbs 16:24 highlights the power of positive words: "Gracious words are a honeycomb, sweet to the soul and healing to the bones." Parents should regularly affirm their children's strengths and accomplishments, providing a foundation of support and love.

Balancing Authority and Compassion

Authority in Parenting

Parents have the God-given authority to guide and direct their children. This authority should be exercised with wisdom, consistency, and firmness. Hebrews 12:11 acknowledges the importance of discipline: "No discipline seems pleasant at the time, but painful. Later on, however, it produces a harvest of righteousness and peace for those who have been trained by it."

Compassion in Parenting

Authority must be balanced with compassion. Colossians 3:21 warns, "Fathers, do not embitter your children, or they will become discouraged." Compassion involves understanding and empathizing with a child's feelings, showing kindness, and being patient with their growth process.

### Challenges and Opportunities

### Navigating Modern Pressures

Modern society presents unique challenges for families, including technological distractions, cultural pressures, and busy schedules. Parents must navigate these challenges with discernment, establishing boundaries and priorities that align with biblical values. This may involve limiting screen time, fostering face-to-face interactions, and creating a family culture centered on faith and love.

### Blended Families and Diverse Dynamics

Blended families and diverse family dynamics require sensitivity and adaptability. Ephesians 4:2 encourages, "Be completely humble and gentle; be patient, bearing with one another in love." Building strong relationships in blended families involves acknowledging and respecting different backgrounds, creating new traditions, and fostering unity.

### Maintaining Love Through Difficult Seasons

Families may face difficult seasons, such as illness, financial hardship, or relational conflicts. During these times, maintaining love and support is crucial. Romans 12:12 advises, "Be joyful in hope, patient in affliction, faithful in prayer." Relying on God's strength, seeking community support, and maintaining open communication can help families navigate these challenges with love.

Practical Applications

Prayer and Spiritual Practices

Incorporating regular prayer and spiritual practices into family life nurtures love and spiritual growth. Families can pray together, read the Bible, and engage in worship. These practices create a spiritual foundation and foster a sense of God's presence in daily life.

Intentional Acts of Love

Demonstrating intentional acts of love strengthens family relationships. This can include writing notes of encouragement, performing acts of service, and celebrating each other's achievements. Intentional acts of love reinforce a culture of appreciation and kindness within the family.

Seeking Support and Guidance

Parents can benefit from seeking support and guidance from other believers, mentors, and pastoral resources. Proverbs 11:14 states, "For lack of guidance a nation falls, but victory is won through many advisers." Engaging in parenting groups, seeking counseling, and attending family workshops can provide valuable insights and encouragement.

Love in the family, grounded in biblical principles, is essential for nurturing healthy, loving relationships in marriage and parenting. By following the biblical foundations for love, practicing mutual submission, sacrificial love, respect, and honor, and nurturing and training children in the ways of the Lord, families can reflect God's love and create a strong, supportive, and spiritually vibrant home.

As we continue to explore the theology of love, let us commit to embodying love in our family relationships. By doing so, we reflect God's character, build strong family bonds, and provide a foundation for the next generation to grow in faith and love. Through intentional practices, open communication, and reliance on God's guidance, we can create loving, nurturing families that honor God and bless one another.

## 5.1.0 PRACTICAL WAYS TO CULTIVATE LOVE WITHIN THE FAMILY

Cultivating love within the family is essential for creating a nurturing and supportive environment where each member can thrive. This chapter explores practical ways to foster love in family relationships, drawing on biblical principles and real-life applications. By intentionally practicing these principles, families can build strong bonds, foster spiritual growth, and reflect the love of Christ.

Daily Practices to Cultivate Love

Regular Family Devotions

Spiritual Growth Together

One of the most effective ways to cultivate love within the family is through regular family devotions. This practice involves setting aside time daily or weekly to read the Bible, pray, and discuss spiritual matters together. Family devotions provide an opportunity for shared spiritual growth and deepen the family's connection with God and each other.

Engaging Activities

Incorporating engaging activities, such as singing worship songs, discussing Bible stories, or watching faith-based videos, can make family devotions more enjoyable and meaningful, especially for children. This practice helps instill spiritual values and encourages open communication about faith.

Expressing Appreciation

Daily Affirmations

Expressing appreciation is a powerful way to cultivate love. Each family member should make a habit of acknowledging and affirming the positive qualities and actions of others. Daily affirmations can include verbal praise, written notes, or small acts of kindness.

Creating a Culture of Gratitude

Creating a culture of gratitude involves regularly expressing thanks for both small and significant contributions. This practice fosters an environment where everyone feels valued and appreciated, strengthening family bonds and promoting a positive atmosphere.

Quality Time

Prioritizing Togetherness

Spending quality time together is crucial for cultivating love in the family. This means prioritizing activities that allow family members to connect and enjoy each other's company. Whether it's shared meals, game nights, or outdoor activities, quality time fosters a sense of belonging and togetherness.

Unplugging from Technology

To make the most of quality time, families should consider unplugging from technology. Setting aside specific times when devices are turned off allows for more meaningful interactions and helps family members focus on each other without distractions.

Open and Honest Communication

Creating Safe Spaces

Open and honest communication is vital for cultivating love and trust within the family. Creating safe spaces where family members feel comfortable sharing their thoughts, feelings, and concerns without fear of judgment is essential. This practice encourages transparency and fosters deeper connections.

Active Listening

Active listening involves fully engaging with the speaker, making eye contact, and responding thoughtfully. By practicing active listening, family members show respect and empathy, demonstrating that they value each other's perspectives.

Building Strong Relationships

Conflict Resolution

Biblical Principles

Conflict is inevitable in any family, but how it is handled can either strengthen or weaken relationships. Ephesians 4:26-27 advises, "In your anger do not sin: Do not let the sun go down while you are still angry, and do not give the devil a foothold." Addressing conflicts promptly and with a spirit of forgiveness is crucial for maintaining harmony.

Practical Steps

Practical steps for resolving conflicts include:

- Identifying the Issue: Clearly define the problem without blaming or accusing.

- Seeking Understanding: Listen to each other's perspectives with empathy and without interrupting.

- Finding Common Ground: Look for areas of agreement and work towards a mutually acceptable solution.

- Forgiving and Moving Forward: Let go of resentment and commit to rebuilding trust and harmony.

Acts of Service

Serving One Another

Acts of service are practical expressions of love that demonstrate care and commitment. Serving one another in everyday tasks, such as cooking, cleaning, or helping with homework, shows that family members are willing to put others' needs above their own.

Encouraging Volunteerism

Encouraging volunteerism within the family can also foster a spirit of service. Participating in community service projects or church activities together helps family members bond while contributing to a greater cause.

Celebrating Milestones and Achievements

Acknowledging Accomplishments

Celebrating milestones and achievements is an important way to cultivate love and build self-esteem. Whether it's a birthday, graduation, or a personal accomplishment, acknowledging and celebrating these events shows appreciation and support.

Creating Traditions

Creating family traditions around these celebrations can strengthen family bonds and create lasting memories. Traditions can include special meals, rituals, or activities that everyone looks forward to and cherishes.

Fostering Emotional and Spiritual Well-being

Providing Emotional Support

Being Present

Providing emotional support involves being present and attentive to each other's needs. This means offering a listening ear, a comforting hug, or words of encouragement during difficult times. Showing empathy and compassion helps family members feel understood and valued.

Encouraging Open Expression

Encouraging open expression of emotions allows family members to share their joys, sorrows, and fears without judgment. This practice fosters emotional intimacy and helps build a supportive and nurturing environment.

Nurturing Spiritual Growth

### Modeling Faith

Parents play a crucial role in nurturing their children's spiritual growth by modeling their faith. Living out Christian values, such as honesty, integrity, and compassion, provides a powerful example for children to follow.

### Providing Spiritual Guidance

Providing spiritual guidance involves teaching children about God, guiding them in prayer, and helping them understand the Bible. Deuteronomy 6:6-7 emphasizes the importance of this role: "These commandments that I give you today are to be on your hearts. Impress them on your children. Talk about them when you sit at home and when you walk along the road, when you lie down and when you get up."

### Strengthening the Family Unit

### Developing a Family Mission Statement

### Defining Values and Goals

Developing a family mission statement can help clarify the family's values and goals. This statement serves as a guiding principle for how the family will live out their faith and love. It can include commitments to spend time together, support one another, and serve the community.

### Revisiting and Reflecting

Revisiting and reflecting on the family mission statement regularly helps ensure that the family remains aligned with their values and goals. It provides an opportunity to celebrate progress, address challenges, and make adjustments as needed.

Encouraging Teamwork

Working Together

Encouraging teamwork within the family fosters a sense of unity and collaboration. Working together on projects, whether it's a home improvement task or planning a family event, helps build cooperation and communication skills.

Celebrating Team Efforts

Celebrating team efforts, regardless of the outcome, reinforces the importance of working together and supporting one another. This practice helps family members appreciate each other's contributions and strengthens the family bond.

Addressing Challenges and Building Resilience

Navigating Difficult Seasons

Relying on Faith

Families will inevitably face difficult seasons, such as illness, financial struggles, or loss. Relying on faith during these times provides strength and hope. Philippians 4:6-7 encourages believers to bring their concerns to God: "Do not be anxious about anything but in every situation, by prayer and petition, with thanksgiving, present your requests to God. And the peace of God, which transcends all understanding, will guard your hearts and your minds in Christ Jesus."

Seeking Support

Seeking support from the church community, friends, and family members can provide additional strength and encouragement. It is important to recognize that asking for help is a sign of wisdom and strength, not weakness.

Building Resilience

Fostering a Positive Outlook

Building resilience involves fostering a positive outlook and focusing on solutions rather than problems. Encouraging family members to look for the silver lining in challenging situations and to trust in God's plan helps build a resilient mindset.

Practicing Gratitude

Practicing gratitude is another way to build resilience. Keeping a gratitude journal or sharing things for which the family is thankful each day helps shift the focus from challenges to blessings, fostering a more positive and resilient attitude.

Cultivating love within the family requires intentionality, effort, and reliance on biblical principles. By practicing regular family devotions, expressing appreciation, spending quality time together, fostering open communication, resolving conflicts constructively, and serving one another, families can build strong, loving relationships that reflect the love of Christ.

As we continue to explore the theology of love, let us commit to implementing these practical ways to cultivate love within our families. By doing so, we create a nurturing and supportive environment where each family member can grow spiritually, emotionally, and relationally. Through intentional practices, open communication, and reliance on God's guidance, we can build loving, resilient families that honor God and bless one another.

## 5.2.0 LOVE IN THE CHURCH

Building a loving and inclusive church community is essential for reflecting the heart of God and advancing His Kingdom on earth. The church is called to be a place where love, unity, and mutual support are evident, providing a compelling witness to the world. This chapter explores biblical principles and practical steps for cultivating a loving and inclusive church community.

Biblical Foundations for Love in the Church

The Greatest Commandment

Jesus identified love as the greatest commandment, central to the life of His followers. In Matthew 22:37-40, He states, "'Love the Lord your God with all your heart and with all your soul and with all your mind.' This is the first and greatest commandment. And the second is like it: 'Love your neighbor as yourself.' All the Law and the Prophets hang on these two commandments." The church, as a community of believers, is called to embody these commandments in its relationships and practices.

The New Commandment

Jesus further emphasized the importance of love in the church by giving a new commandment in John 13:34-35: "A new command I give you: Love one another. As I have loved you, so you must love one another. By this everyone will know that you are my disciples if you love one another." This commandment highlights that love is the distinguishing mark of Christ's disciples and should be evident in the church community.

The Early Church Model

The early church provides a powerful model of a loving and inclusive community. Acts 2:42-47 describes the early believers' commitment to fellowship, shared meals, prayer, and mutual support: "They devoted themselves to the apostles' teaching and to fellowship, to the breaking of bread and to prayer... All the believers were together and had everything in common. They sold property and possessions to give to anyone who had need." This model illustrates the practical expression of love and inclusivity in the church.

Principles for Building a Loving Church Community

Unity in Diversity

Embracing Diversity

The church is called to embrace diversity, recognizing that believers come from different backgrounds, cultures, and experiences. Galatians 3:28 affirms, "There is neither Jew nor Gentile, neither slave nor free, nor is there male and female, for you are all one in Christ Jesus." Embracing diversity involves valuing each person's unique contributions and creating an inclusive environment where everyone feels welcome.

Promoting Unity

Unity is essential for a loving church community. Ephesians 4:3 encourages believers to "make every effort to keep the unity of the Spirit through the bond of peace." Promoting unity involves fostering mutual respect, resolving conflicts constructively, and focusing on shared faith and mission.

Mutual Support and Encouragement

Bearing One Another's Burdens

Mutual support and encouragement are vital aspects of a loving church community. Galatians 6:2 instructs, "Carry each other's burdens, and in this way, you will fulfill the law of Christ." This involves providing practical assistance, emotional support, and spiritual encouragement to those in need.

Encouraging One Another

Hebrews 10:24-25 emphasizes the importance of encouragement: "And let us consider how we may spur one another on toward love and good deeds, not giving up meeting together, as some are in the habit of doing, but encouraging one another—and all the more as you see the Day approaching." Encouraging one another involves offering words of affirmation, praying for each other, and celebrating successes and milestones.

Servant Leadership

Following Christ's Example

Servant leadership, modeled by Jesus, is foundational for a loving church community. In Mark 10:45, Jesus declares, "For even the Son of Man did not come to be served, but to serve, and to give His life as a ransom for many." Church leaders are called to follow Christ's example by serving others with humility and selflessness.

Empowering Others

Servant leadership involves empowering others to use their gifts and talents for the benefit of the church. Ephesians 4:11-12 explains, "So Christ Himself gave the apostles, the prophets, the evangelists, the pastors, and teachers, to equip His people for works of service, so that the body of Christ may be built up." Empowering others fosters a sense of ownership and participation, strengthening the church community.

Intentional Inclusivity

Welcoming All

A loving church community intentionally welcomes all people, regardless of their background or circumstances. Romans 15:7 urges, "Accept one another, then, just as Christ accepted you, in order to bring praise to God." This involves creating a welcoming atmosphere, offering hospitality, and actively reaching out to newcomers and those on the margins.

Addressing Barriers to Inclusion

Addressing barriers to inclusion is crucial for building a loving church community. This may involve examining and addressing issues such as language barriers, accessibility, and cultural differences. By identifying and removing these barriers, the church can create a more inclusive environment where everyone feels valued and included.

Practical Steps for Cultivating Love in the Church

Fostering Authentic Relationships

Small Groups and Fellowship

Small groups and fellowship activities provide opportunities for building authentic relationships within the church. These settings allow for deeper connections, mutual support, and accountability. Acts 2:46 highlights the early church's practice of gathering in small groups: "They broke bread in their homes and ate together with glad and sincere hearts."

Mentorship and Discipleship

Mentorship and discipleship programs help cultivate love and spiritual growth within the church. Experienced believers can guide and support others in their faith journey, fostering a culture of mutual care and growth. 2 Timothy 2:2 emphasizes the importance of discipleship: "And the things you have heard me say in the presence of many witnesses entrust to reliable people who will also be qualified to teach others."

Practicing Hospitality

Welcoming Strangers

Hospitality is a practical expression of love in the church. Hebrews 13:2 encourages, "Do not forget to show hospitality to strangers, for by so doing some people have shown hospitality to angels without knowing it." Practicing hospitality involves inviting newcomers into the church community, hosting meals, and creating a welcoming environment.

Caring for the Vulnerable

Hospitality also includes caring for the vulnerable and marginalized. James 1:27 reminds us, "Religion that God our Father accepts as pure and faultless is this: to look after orphans and widows in their distress and to keep oneself from being polluted by the world." The church can demonstrate love by providing support and resources to those in need.

Engaging in Acts of Service

Serving the Community

Engaging in acts of service within the community reflects the love of Christ. The church can organize service projects, partner with local organizations, and meet the practical needs of those in the community. Matthew 25:35-36 emphasizes the importance of serving others: "For I was hungry and you gave me something to eat, I was thirsty and you gave me something to drink, I was a stranger and you invited me in, I needed clothes and you clothed me, I was sick and you looked after me, I was in prison and you came to visit me."

Encouraging Volunteerism

Encouraging volunteerism within the church helps foster a culture of service and love. Providing opportunities for members to use their gifts and talents in service to others strengthens the church community and reflects the love of Christ.

Promoting Open Communication

Transparency and Trust

Promoting open communication within the church fosters transparency and trust. Leaders should communicate openly about church decisions, finances, and vision, inviting input and feedback from the congregation. Proverbs 27:17 highlights the value of mutual sharpening: "As iron sharpens iron, so one person sharpens another."

Resolving Conflicts Constructively

Resolving conflicts constructively is essential for maintaining a loving church community. Matthew 18:15-17 provides a biblical framework for addressing conflicts: "If your brother or sister sins, go and point out their fault, just between the two of you. If they listen to you, you have won them over." Addressing conflicts with a spirit of humility and reconciliation promotes unity and peace.

Challenges and Opportunities

Navigating Cultural Differences

Embracing Multiculturalism

Navigating cultural differences within the church can be challenging but also presents opportunities for growth and enrichment. Embracing multiculturalism involves recognizing and celebrating the diverse cultural expressions within the church. Revelation 7:9 envisions a diverse worship community: "After this, I looked, and there before me was a great multitude that no one could count, from every nation, tribe, people, and language, standing before the throne and before the Lamb."

Promoting Cultural Sensitivity

Promoting cultural sensitivity involves educating the congregation about different cultures and encouraging respect and understanding. This practice helps create an inclusive environment where everyone feels valued and respected.

Addressing Social and Economic Disparities

Providing Support and Resources

Addressing social and economic disparities within the church involves providing support and resources to those in need. This can include financial assistance, job training, and educational opportunities. Acts 4:34-35 describes the early church's approach to economic disparity: "There were no needy persons among them. For from time to time those who owned land or houses sold them, brought the money from the sales and put it at the apostles' feet, and it was distributed to anyone who had need."

Advocating for Justice

The church can also advocate for justice and work towards systemic change to address social and economic disparities. This involves speaking out against injustice, partnering with advocacy organizations, and engaging in community development efforts.

Building a loving and inclusive church community is essential for reflecting the heart of God and advancing His Kingdom on earth. By embracing diversity, promoting unity, providing mutual support, practicing servant leadership, and fostering authentic relationships, the church can create an environment where love and inclusivity flourish.

As we continue to explore the theology of love, let us commit to implementing these practical steps to cultivate love within our church communities. By doing so, we create a welcoming and supportive environment where each member can grow spiritually, emotionally, and relationally. Through intentional practices, open communication, and reliance on God's guidance, we can build loving, resilient church communities that honor God and bless one another.

## 5.2.1 THE ROLE OF LOVE IN CHURCH LEADERSHIP AND MINISTRY T

Love is a fundamental element in church leadership and ministry. It shapes the way leaders serve, influences how ministry is conducted, and impacts the overall health and growth of the church community. This chapter explores the role of love in church leadership and ministry, emphasizing biblical principles and practical applications to foster a loving and effective church environment.

Biblical Foundations for Love in Leadership

Jesus as the Model of Loving Leadership

Jesus Christ is the ultimate model of loving leadership. His ministry was marked by compassion, humility, and self-sacrifice. In John 13:34-35, Jesus commands His disciples, "A new command I give you: Love one another. As I have loved you, so you must love one another. By this everyone will know that you are my disciples if you love one another." Jesus' leadership was defined by love, setting an example for all church leaders to follow.

The Apostle Paul's Example

The Apostle Paul also exemplified loving leadership. In 1 Thessalonians 2:7-8, Paul writes, "Instead, we were like young children among you. Just as a nursing mother cares for her children, so we care for you. Because we loved you so much, we were delighted to share with you not only the gospel of God but our lives as well." Paul's ministry was characterized by deep affection and personal investment in the lives of those he served.

Principles of Loving Leadership

Servant Leadership

Following Christ's Example

Servant leadership is central to loving leadership in the church. Jesus taught that true leadership is about serving others rather than seeking power or status. In Mark 10:42-45, Jesus explains, "You know that those who are regarded as rulers of the Gentiles lord it over them, and their high officials exercise authority over them. Not so with you. Instead, whoever wants to become great among you must be your servant, and whoever wants to be first must be the slave of all. For even the Son of Man did not come to be served, but to serve, and to give His life as a ransom for many."

Empowering and Equipping Others

Servant leaders focus on empowering and equipping others for ministry. Ephesians 4:11-12 states, "So Christ Himself gave the apostles, the prophets, the evangelists, the pastors, and teachers, to equip His people for works of service, so that the body of Christ may be built up." Loving leaders invest in the growth and development of their congregation, enabling them to use their gifts and talents for the benefit of the church.

Humility and Compassion

Leading with Humility

Humility is a key characteristic of loving leadership. Philippians 2:3-4 instructs, "Do nothing out of selfish ambition or vain conceit. Rather, in humility value others above yourselves, not looking to your own interests but each of you to the interests of the others." Humble leaders prioritize the needs and well-being of others, fostering a culture of mutual respect and care.

Demonstrating Compassion

Compassion is another essential quality of loving leadership. Colossians 3:12 encourages, "Therefore, as God's chosen people, holy and dearly loved, clothe yourselves with compassion, kindness, humility, gentleness, and patience." Compassionate leaders are attentive to the struggles and needs of their congregation, offering support and encouragement.

Practical Applications of Love in Leadership

Building Relationships

Personal Connection

Loving leaders prioritize building personal connections with their congregation. This involves getting to know individuals, understanding their needs, and being present in their lives. Personal connection fosters trust and a sense of belonging within the church community.

Mentorship and Discipleship

Mentorship and discipleship are practical ways to build relationships and foster spiritual growth. Leaders can mentor emerging leaders, provide guidance, and model Christ-like behavior. 2 Timothy 2:2 highlights the importance of discipleship: "And the things you have heard me say in the presence of many witnesses entrust to reliable people who will also be qualified to teach others."

Creating a Supportive Environment

Encouraging and Affirming

Creating a supportive environment involves encouraging and affirming church members. 1 Thessalonians 5:11 urges, "Therefore encourage one another and build each other up, just as in fact you are doing." Encouragement boosts morale and fosters a positive atmosphere within the church.

Providing Resources and Opportunities

Loving leaders ensure that church members have the resources and opportunities they need to grow and serve. This includes offering educational programs, training workshops, and opportunities for involvement in various ministries. Providing resources empowers individuals and helps them develop their potential.

Fostering Unity and Collaboration

Promoting Teamwork

Unity and collaboration are vital for a healthy church environment. Ephesians 4:3 encourages, "Make every effort to keep the unity of the Spirit through the bond of peace." Loving leaders promote teamwork, encouraging members to work together harmoniously for the common good.

Resolving Conflicts Constructively

Conflicts are inevitable, but loving leaders address them constructively. Matthew 18:15-17 provides guidance on resolving conflicts: "If your brother or sister sins, go and point out their fault, just between the two of you. If they listen to you, you have won them over." Leaders should facilitate open communication and reconciliation, fostering a culture of forgiveness and understanding.

The Role of Love in Ministry

Preaching and Teaching with Love

Communicating God's Love

Preaching and teaching are central to ministry, and these activities should be infused with love. Ephesians 4:15 emphasizes the importance of speaking the truth in love: "Instead, speaking the truth in love, we will grow to become in every respect the mature body of Him who is the head, that is, Christ." Communicating God's love through sermons and lessons helps build up the congregation and draws people closer to Christ.

### Addressing Needs with Sensitivity

Loving ministry involves addressing the spiritual, emotional, and practical needs of the congregation with sensitivity. This means being aware of the challenges people face and offering relevant, compassionate guidance and support.

### Pastoral Care and Counseling

### Providing Support

Pastoral care and counseling are critical aspects of loving ministry. Leaders provide support during times of crisis, offering comfort and guidance. James 5:14-15 underscores the importance of pastoral care: "Is anyone among you sick? Let them call the elders of the church to pray over them and anoint them with oil in the name of the Lord. And the prayer offered in faith will make the sick person well; the Lord will raise them up."

### Offering Hope and Healing

In pastoral counseling, leaders offer hope and healing through prayer, scripture, and empathetic listening. They help individuals navigate personal challenges, providing a safe space for sharing and healing.

### Community Outreach and Service

Serving the Wider Community

Loving ministry extends beyond the church walls to serve the wider community. Acts 1:8 calls believers to be witnesses "in Jerusalem, and in all Judea and Samaria, and to the ends of the earth." Community outreach initiatives, such as food drives, health clinics, and educational programs, demonstrate Christ's love in practical ways.

Building Partnerships

Building partnerships with local organizations and other churches enhances the church's ability to serve the community. Collaboration amplifies the impact of outreach efforts and fosters a spirit of unity and cooperation.

Challenges in Loving Leadership and Ministry

Balancing Responsibilities

Avoiding Burnout

One of the challenges in loving leadership and ministry is balancing responsibilities and avoiding burnout. Leaders must manage their time and energy wisely, setting boundaries and prioritizing self-care. Mark 6:31 highlights the importance of rest: "Then, because so many people were coming and going that they did not even have a chance to eat, He said to them, 'Come with Me by yourselves to a quiet place and get some rest.'"

Delegating Tasks

Delegating tasks to capable individuals within the church helps distribute the workload and prevents burnout. It also empowers others to develop their leadership skills and contribute to the ministry.

Navigating Criticism and Opposition

Responding with Grace

Leaders and ministers may face criticism and opposition. Responding with grace and humility is crucial. Romans 12:18 advises, "If it is possible, as far as it depends on you, live at peace with everyone." Handling criticism constructively and maintaining a loving attitude helps preserve unity and integrity.

Seeking Wise Counsel

Seeking wise counsel from trusted mentors and peers can provide perspective and support during challenging times. Proverbs 11:14 states, "For lack of guidance a nation falls, but victory is won through many advisers." Consulting others helps leaders navigate difficulties with wisdom and strength.

Love is central to effective church leadership and ministry. By following the example of Jesus and the Apostle Paul, leaders can cultivate a culture of love, humility, and service within the church. Practical applications such as building relationships, creating a supportive environment, fostering unity, and engaging in community outreach demonstrate love in action and strengthen the church community.

As we continue to explore the theology of love, let us commit to integrating love into every aspect of church leadership and ministry. By doing so, we reflect the heart of God, build up the body of Christ, and provide a compelling witness to the world. Through intentional practices, open communication, and reliance on God's guidance, we can create loving, effective church communities that honor God and bless one another.

## 5.2.2 LOVE IN SOCIETY

Jesus' teaching in Matthew 5:43-48 calls believers to love not only their neighbors but also their enemies. This radical love challenges societal norms and reflects the heart of God. This chapter explores the biblical foundations and practical applications of loving our neighbors and enemies, emphasizing how this commandment can transform society and reflect the Kingdom of God.

Biblical Foundations for Loving Neighbors and Enemies

The Greatest Commandment

Jesus emphasized the importance of loving our neighbors as part of the greatest commandment. In Matthew

22:37-40, He says, "'Love the Lord your God with all your heart and with all your soul and with all your mind.' This is the first and greatest commandment. And the second is like it: 'Love your neighbor as yourself.' All the Law and the Prophets hang on these two commandments." Loving our neighbors is a fundamental aspect of our faith and obedience to God.

Love for Enemies

Jesus' teaching in Matthew 5:43-48 extends the command to love beyond our neighbors to include our enemies: "You have heard that it was said, 'Love your neighbor and hate your enemy.' But I tell you, love your enemies and pray for those who persecute you, that you may be children of your Father in heaven. He causes His sun to rise on the evil and the good, and sends rain on the righteous and the unrighteous. If you love those who love you, what reward will you get? Are not even the tax collectors doing that? And if you greet only your own people, what are you doing more than others? Do not even pagans do that? Be perfect, therefore, as your heavenly Father is perfect."

This passage calls believers to a higher standard of love, one that reflects the nature of God, who loves all people without partiality.

Theological Reflections on Loving Neighbors and Enemies

Imitating God's Love

Unconditional Love

God's love is unconditional, extended to both the righteous and the unrighteous. By loving our neighbors and enemies, we imitate God's love and reflect His character. 1 John 4:19 emphasizes, "We love because He first loved us." Our capacity to love others, including our enemies, flows from our experience of God's love.

Perfect Love

Jesus' call to "be perfect, therefore, as your heavenly Father is perfect" (Matthew 5:48) highlights the aspiration for believers to love completely and without discrimination. This perfection in love involves striving to love others as God loves us, even when it is difficult.

Breaking Down Barriers

Overcoming Prejudice

Loving our neighbors and enemies involves overcoming prejudices and breaking down societal barriers. Galatians 3:28 declares, "There is neither Jew nor Gentile, neither slave nor free, nor is there male and female, for you are all one in Christ Jesus." The love of Christ transcends social, cultural, and ethnic divisions, calling believers to see all people as created in God's image and deserving of love and respect.

Promoting Reconciliation

Reconciliation is a key aspect of loving our enemies. 2 Corinthians 5:18-19 teaches, "All this is from God, who reconciled us to Himself through Christ and gave us the ministry of reconciliation: that God was reconciling the world to Himself in Christ, not counting people's sins against them. And He has committed to us the message of reconciliation." Loving our enemies involves seeking reconciliation and peace, reflecting God's desire for harmony and unity.

Practical Steps for Loving Neighbors and Enemies

Cultivating Compassion and Empathy

Understanding Others

Cultivating compassion and empathy involves understanding the experiences and perspectives of others. Philippians 2:4 advises, "Not looking to your own interests but each of you to the interests of the others." By actively listening and seeking to understand others, we demonstrate love and build bridges of empathy.

Praying for Others

Prayer is a powerful way to cultivate love for our neighbors and enemies. Jesus instructs us to pray for those who persecute us (Matthew 5:44). Praying for others, especially those who have wronged us, softens our hearts and aligns our attitudes with God's love.

Acts of Kindness and Service

Serving All People

Acts of kindness and service are tangible expressions of love. Galatians 6:10 encourages, "Therefore, as we have opportunity, let us do good to all people, especially to those who belong to the family of believers." Serving our neighbors and enemies through acts of kindness demonstrates the love of Christ and has the potential to transform relationships.

Meeting Needs

Meeting the practical needs of others, such as providing food, clothing, or assistance, is a way to love our neighbors and enemies. James 2:15-17 challenges believers to demonstrate their faith through action: "Suppose a brother or a sister is without clothes and daily food. If one of you says to them, 'Go in peace; keep warm and well fed,' but does nothing about their physical needs, what good is it? In the same way, faith by itself, if it is not accompanied by action, is dead."

Forgiveness and Reconciliation

Extending Forgiveness

Forgiveness is essential for loving our enemies. Colossians 3:13 instructs, "Bear with each other and forgive one another if any of you has a grievance against someone.

Forgive as the Lord forgave you." Forgiving those who have wronged us frees us from bitterness and allows God's love to flow through us.

Pursuing Reconciliation

Pursuing reconciliation involves actively seeking to restore broken relationships. Romans 12:18 encourages, "If it is possible, as far as it depends on you, live at peace with everyone." This requires humility, patience, and a willingness to engage in difficult conversations for the sake of peace.

Advocating for Justice and Equity

Standing Against Injustice

Loving our neighbors and enemies includes advocating for justice and equity. Micah 6:8 calls believers to "act justly and to love mercy and to walk humbly with your God." This involves standing against injustice, speaking out for the oppressed, and working towards systemic change.

Promoting Equity

Promoting equity involves creating opportunities and removing barriers for marginalized groups. Proverbs 31:8-9 urges, "Speak up for those who cannot speak for themselves, for the rights of all who are destitute. Speak up and judge fairly; defend the rights of the poor and needy." By advocating for equitable treatment and opportunities, believers demonstrate the inclusive love of God.

Engaging in Peacemaking

Building Bridges

Peacemaking is a proactive way to love our neighbors and enemies. Matthew 5:9 blesses peacemakers: "Blessed are the peacemakers, for they will be called children of God." Building bridges between divided communities and fostering dialogue and understanding promotes peace and reconciliation.

Conflict Resolution

Engaging in conflict resolution helps to address and heal divisions. 1 Peter 3:11 encourages, "They must turn from evil and do good; they must seek peace and pursue it." By actively resolving conflicts and promoting peaceful interactions, believers contribute to a more harmonious society.

Challenges in Loving Neighbors and Enemies

Overcoming Fear and Prejudice

Relying on God's Strength

Loving neighbors and enemies can be challenging due to fear and prejudice. Relying on God's strength and guidance helps believers overcome these barriers. 2 Timothy 1:7 reminds us, "For the Spirit God gave us does not make us timid, but gives us power, love, and self-discipline." Trusting in God's empowerment enables us to love courageously.

### Educating Ourselves

Educating ourselves about different cultures, experiences, and perspectives helps to dismantle prejudices and fosters empathy. By seeking to understand and learn, believers can approach others with an open heart and mind.

### Persisting in Love

### Consistency in Action

Persisting in love requires consistency and perseverance, even when it is difficult. Galatians 6:9 encourages, "Let us not become weary in doing good, for at the proper time we will reap a harvest if we do not give up." By continuing to love and serve others faithfully, we reflect the steadfast love of God.

### Trusting in God's Timing

Trusting in God's timing involves recognizing that change and reconciliation may take time. Isaiah 40:31 reassures, "But those who hope in the Lord will renew their strength. They will soar on wings like eagles; they will run and not grow weary, they will walk and not be faint." Patience and trust in God's plan are essential for loving our neighbors and enemies effectively.

### The Impact of Love in Society

### Transforming Relationships

### Healing Divisions

Loving our neighbors and enemies has the power to heal divisions and transform relationships. Ephesians 2:14-16 speaks of Christ breaking down the dividing wall of hostility: "For He Himself is our peace, who has made the two groups one and has destroyed the barrier, the dividing wall of hostility." By practicing love, believers can contribute to reconciliation and unity in society.

Building Community

Love fosters a sense of community and belonging. Acts 4:32 describes the early church's communal love: "All the believers were one in heart and mind. No one claimed that any of their possessions was their own, but they shared everything they had." Building a loving community reflects the Kingdom of God and provides a powerful witness to the world.

Reflecting the Kingdom of God

Demonstrating God's Love

Loving our neighbors and enemies demonstrates God's love for the world. John 13:35 states, "By this everyone will know that you are my disciples, if you love one another." Through

acts of love, believers reflect the character of God and draw others to Him.

Advancing God's Kingdom

Advancing God's Kingdom involves living out the values of love, justice, and reconciliation. Matthew 6:10 prays, "Your kingdom come, you will be done, on earth as it is in heaven." By embodying these values, believers contribute to the realization of God's Kingdom on earth.

Loving our neighbors and enemies, as taught by Jesus in Matthew 5:43-48, is a radical and transformative commandment. It calls believers to reflect God's unconditional love, break down societal barriers, and actively seek reconciliation and justice. Through practical steps such as cultivating compassion, serving others, forgiving, and advocating for equity, believers can demonstrate the love of Christ in society.

As we continue to explore the theology of love, let us commit to loving our neighbors and enemies with the same unconditional and sacrificial love that God has shown us. By doing so, we can transform relationships, build a sense of community, and advance the Kingdom of God on earth. Through intentional actions, open hearts, and reliance on God's strength, we can create a more loving and just society that honors God and reflects His love for the world.

## 5.3.0 CHRISTIAN LOVE AS A CATALYST FOR SOCIAL CHANGE

Christian love, rooted in the teachings of Jesus and the principles of the Gospel, has the transformative power to effect significant social change. By embodying the love of Christ in actions and attitudes, believers can address injustices, foster reconciliation, and build communities that reflect the values of the Kingdom of God. This chapter explores how Christian love acts as a catalyst for social change, examining biblical foundations, historical examples, and practical applications for contemporary society.

Biblical Foundations for Social Change Through Love

The Mission of Jesus

Jesus' ministry was characterized by a profound commitment to social transformation through love. Luke 4:18-19 encapsulates His mission: "The Spirit of the Lord is on me because he has anointed me to proclaim good news to the poor. He has sent me to proclaim freedom for the prisoners and recovery of sight for the blind, to set the oppressed free, to proclaim the year of the Lord's favor." Jesus' life and teachings consistently demonstrated love for the marginalized and a challenge to unjust structures.

The Parable of the Good Samaritan

The Parable of the Good Samaritan (Luke 10:25-37) provides a powerful example of love in action, crossing social boundaries to offer help and compassion. Jesus concludes the parable with the command to "go and do likewise," calling His followers to extend love beyond cultural and social divisions to those in need.

The Early Church

The early church exemplified love-driven social change. Acts 2:44-45 describes their communal lifestyle: "All the believers were together and had everything in common. They sold property and possessions to give to anyone who had need." This radical expression of love and generosity addressed economic disparities and fostered a sense of unity and mutual support.

Historical Examples of Christian Love Driving Social Change

Abolition of Slavery

William Wilberforce and the Clapham Sect

Christian love played a crucial role in the abolition of slavery, particularly through the efforts of William Wilberforce and the Clapham Sect in the 18th and 19th centuries. Motivated by their Christian faith and the belief in the inherent dignity of all people, they tirelessly campaigned against the transatlantic slave trade, leading to the passage of the Slave Trade Act of 1807 and the Slavery Abolition Act of 1833 in the British Empire.

Harriet Tubman and the Underground Railroad

In the United States, Harriet Tubman, a devout Christian, exemplified love-driven activism through her work with the Underground Railroad. Her faith inspired her to risk her life repeatedly to lead enslaved people to freedom, demonstrating the power of Christian love in action.

Civil Rights Movement

Martin Luther King Jr.

The Civil Rights Movement in the United States was deeply rooted in Christian principles of love and justice. Martin Luther King Jr., a Baptist minister, advocated for nonviolent resistance and civil disobedience based on the teachings of Jesus. His famous "I Have a Dream" speech and leadership in the movement exemplified how Christian love could challenge systemic racism and promote equality.

Desmond Tutu and Apartheid

In South Africa, Archbishop Desmond Tutu played a significant role in the struggle against apartheid. Grounded in his Christian faith, Tutu advocated for justice, reconciliation, and forgiveness, emphasizing the power of love to overcome hatred and division.

Principles for Love-Driven Social Change

Compassion and Empathy

Understanding and Relating

Christian love requires compassion and empathy—understanding and relating to the suffering of others. Hebrews 13:3 urges, "Continue to remember those in prison as if you were together with them in prison, and those who are mistreated as if you yourselves were suffering." This perspective fosters a deep connection and commitment to addressing the needs of others.

Practical Compassion

Compassion must translate into practical actions. Matthew 25:35-36 highlights the importance of meeting tangible needs: "For I was hungry and you gave me something to eat, I was thirsty and you gave me something to drink, I was a stranger and you invited me in, I needed clothes and you clothed me, I was sick and you looked after me, I was in prison and you came to visit me." Addressing basic human needs is a fundamental expression of Christian love.

Advocacy and Justice

Speaking Out

Christian love compels believers to speak out against injustice and advocate for those who cannot speak for themselves. Proverbs 31:8-9 commands, "Speak up for those who cannot speak for themselves, for the rights of all who are destitute. Speak up and judge fairly; defend the rights of the poor and needy." Advocacy involves raising awareness, influencing policy, and challenging unjust systems.

Promoting Equity

Promoting equity means ensuring that everyone has access to opportunities and resources, particularly those who have been historically marginalized. Isaiah 1:17 calls for active pursuit of justice: "Learn to do right; seek justice. Defend the oppressed. Take up the cause of the fatherless; plead the case of the widow." Equity-driven initiatives reflect the inclusive love of God.

Reconciliation and Peacebuilding

Forgiveness and Healing

Reconciliation is a central aspect of Christian love, involving forgiveness and the healing of broken relationships. 2 Corinthians 5:18-19 speaks of the ministry of reconciliation: "All this is from God, who reconciled us to Himself through Christ and gave us the ministry of reconciliation: that God was reconciling the world to Himself in Christ, not counting people's sins against them. And He has committed to us the message of reconciliation." Pursuing reconciliation promotes peace and unity.

Building Bridges

Building bridges between divided communities is essential for social change. Ephesians 2:14 emphasizes that

Christ has broken down the dividing wall of hostility: "For He Himself is our peace, who has made the two groups one and has destroyed the barrier, the dividing wall of hostility." Efforts to foster dialogue, understanding, and cooperation can lead to lasting social transformation.

Practical Steps for Christians to Foster Social Change

Engaging in Community Service

Volunteer Work

Engaging in community service is a practical way to demonstrate Christian love and effect social change. Volunteer work in local shelters, food banks, and community centers addresses immediate needs and builds relationships. James 2:14-17 highlights the importance of action: "What good is it, my brothers and sisters if someone claims to have faith but has no deeds? Can such faith save them? Suppose a brother or a sister is without clothes and daily food. If one of you says to them, 'Go in peace; keep warm and well fed,' but does nothing about their physical needs, what good is it? In the same way, faith by itself, if it is not accompanied by action, is dead."

Church-Led Initiatives

Churches can organize and support initiatives that address community needs, such as health clinics, educational programs, and support groups. These efforts reflect the love of Christ and build a positive presence in the community.

Educational and Awareness Campaigns

Raising Awareness

Educational and awareness campaigns can inform and mobilize people to address social issues. By providing information, hosting workshops, and facilitating discussions, churches can raise awareness about injustices and inspire action. Hosea 4:6 emphasizes the importance of knowledge: "My people are destroyed from lack of knowledge."

Collaborating with Organizations

Collaborating with local and global organizations amplifies efforts to effect social change. Partnerships can provide additional resources, expertise, and support, enhancing the impact of initiatives.

Advocacy and Policy Change

Engaging in Advocacy

Christians can engage in advocacy by writing letters to legislators, participating in peaceful protests, and joining advocacy groups. Advocacy efforts aim to influence policy and promote justice. Micah 6:8 calls for active engagement: "He has shown you, O mortal, what is good. And what does the Lord require of you? To act justly and to love mercy and to walk humbly with your God."

### Supporting Fair Policies

Supporting policies that promote justice and equity aligns with Christian love. Believers can use their voices and votes to advocate for legislation that addresses poverty, inequality, and other social issues.

### Peacemaking and Conflict Resolution

### Facilitating Dialogue

Peacemaking involves facilitating dialogue between conflicting parties. Churches can host forums, mediation sessions, and peacebuilding workshops to address and resolve conflicts. Matthew 5:9 blesses peacemakers: "Blessed are the peacemakers, for they will be called children of God."

### Promoting Restorative Justice

Restorative justice focuses on healing and reconciliation rather than punishment. Implementing restorative practices within communities and institutions fosters a more compassionate and just society. Romans 12:17-18 encourages peaceful resolution: "Do not repay anyone evil for evil. Be careful to do what is right in the eyes of everyone. If it is possible, as far as it depends on you, live at peace with everyone."

### Challenges and Opportunities

### Overcoming Resistance

### Addressing Opposition

Efforts to effect social change may encounter resistance and opposition. Christians must be prepared to address challenges with patience, wisdom, and perseverance. 1 Peter 3:15-16 advises, "But in your hearts revere Christ as Lord. Always be prepared to give an answer to everyone who asks you to give the reason for the hope that you have. But do this with gentleness and respect, keeping a clear conscience, so that those who speak maliciously against your good behavior in Christ may be ashamed of their slander."

Relying on God's Strength

Relying on God's strength and guidance is essential in overcoming resistance. Isaiah 40:31 reassures, "But those who hope in the Lord will renew their strength. They will soar on wings like eagles; they will run and not grow weary, they will walk and not be faint."

Sustaining Efforts

Long-Term Commitment

Social change requires long-term commitment and sustained efforts. Christians must remain dedicated to the cause, even when progress seems slow. Galatians 6:9 encourages perseverance: "Let us not become weary in doing good, for at the proper time we will reap a harvest if we do not give up."

Building Networks

Building networks and alliances with other like-minded individuals and organizations enhance sustainability. Collaborative efforts can share resources, provide mutual support, and maintain momentum.

The Impact of Christian Love on Society

Transforming Communities

Addressing Root Causes

Christian love addresses not only the symptoms but also the root causes of social issues. By tackling systemic problems such as poverty, discrimination, and injustice, believers can create lasting positive change in communities.

Fostering Unity

Love fosters unity and reconciliation, breaking down barriers and building inclusive communities. John 13:35 highlights the power of love: "By this, everyone will know that you are my disciples if you love one another." A united community reflects the Kingdom of God and serves as a powerful testimony to the world.

Reflecting the Kingdom of God

Demonstrating God's Love

Acts of love and justice demonstrate God's love and advance His Kingdom on earth. Matthew 6:10 prays, "Your kingdom come, you will be done, on earth as it is in heaven."

By living out these values, believers contribute to the realization of God's Kingdom.

Inspiring Others

Christian love inspires others to join in the work of social change. The witness of believers living out their faith through love can attract others to Christ and mobilize broader support for justice and reconciliation efforts.

Christian love has the transformative power to act as a catalyst for social change. Rooted in the teachings of Jesus and the principles of the Gospel, this love challenges injustices, fosters reconciliation, and builds communities that reflect the values of the Kingdom of God. Through compassion, advocacy, reconciliation, and practical actions, believers can address societal issues and create lasting positive change.

As we continue to explore the theology of love, let us commit to using Christian love as a force for social change. By doing so, we reflect God's heart, advance His Kingdom, and inspire others to join in the work of justice and reconciliation. Through intentional efforts, collaboration, and reliance on God's strength, we can build a more just and loving society that honors God and blesses all people.

# CHAPTER 06

---

## CHALLENGES TO LOVING

### 6.1. Overcoming Selfishness and Pride

Selfishness and pride are significant barriers to loving others as Christ calls us to do. These attitudes hinder our ability to genuinely care for others and create divisions in relationships. This chapter explores the nature of selfishness and pride, their impact on our ability to love, and practical steps for overcoming these barriers to cultivate a more loving and Christ-like life.

Understanding Selfishness and Pride

The Nature of Selfishness

Self-Centeredness

Selfishness is characterized by an excessive focus on oneself and one's own needs, desires, and interests. It manifests in behaviors that prioritize personal gain over the well-being of others. Philippians 2:3 warns against this attitude: "Do nothing out of selfish ambition or vain conceit. Rather, in humility value others above yourselves."

Lack of Empathy

Selfishness often involves a lack of empathy and concern for others. It can lead to neglecting the needs and feelings of those around us, resulting in broken relationships and a lack of genuine connection.

The Nature of Pride

Arrogance and Superiority

Pride involves an inflated sense of self-importance and a desire to be seen as superior to others. Proverbs 16:18 warns, "Pride goes before destruction, a haughty spirit before a fall." This attitude can lead to arrogance and a disdainful attitude toward others.

Resistance to Correction

Pride makes it difficult to accept correction and feedback from others. Proverbs 12:15 states, "The way of fools seems right to them, but the wise listen to advice." This resistance can hinder personal growth and damage relationships.

The Impact of Selfishness and Pride on Love

Hindering Relationships

Creating Division

Selfishness and pride create division and conflict in relationships. When individuals prioritize their own needs and desires over others, it leads to misunderstandings, resentment, and a lack of trust. James 4:1-2 asks, "What causes fights and quarrels among you? Don't they come from your desires that battle within you?"

Blocking Genuine Connection

These attitudes block genuine connection and intimacy. Love requires vulnerability, empathy, and a willingness to prioritize others. Selfishness and pride make it difficult to develop these qualities, resulting in shallow and superficial relationships.

Obstructing Spiritual Growth

Stifling Humility

Humility is essential for spiritual growth and for loving others authentically. 1 Peter 5:5 exhorts, "All of you, clothe yourselves with humility toward one another, because, 'God opposes the proud but shows favor to the humble.'" Selfishness and pride stifle humility, preventing believers from growing in Christ-likeness.

Limiting God's Work

Selfishness and pride limit God's work in our lives. These attitudes create a barrier to receiving God's grace and guidance. Isaiah 66:2 says, "These are the ones I look on with favor: those who are humble and contrite in spirit, and who tremble at my word." A humble and contrite heart is open to God's transformative work.

Identifying Barriers to Love

Self-Examination

Reflecting on Motives

Identifying barriers to love begins with self-examination. Reflecting on our motives and behaviors helps us recognize areas where selfishness and pride may be present. Psalm 139:23-24 invites this introspection: "Search me, God, and know my heart; test me and know my anxious thoughts. See if there is any offensive way in me, and lead me in the way everlasting."

Seeking Feedback

Seeking feedback from trusted friends, family, or mentors can provide valuable insights into how selfishness and pride may be affecting our relationships. Proverbs 27:6 states, "Wounds from a friend can be trusted, but an enemy multiplies kisses." Honest feedback helps us see blind spots and areas for growth.

Practicing Self-Awareness

Mindfulness

Practicing mindfulness involves being present and aware of our thoughts, feelings, and actions. This awareness helps us recognize when selfish or prideful attitudes arise and allows us to address them promptly.

Accountability

Accountability involves inviting others to help us stay mindful of our attitudes and behaviors. Joining a small group or finding an accountability partner provides support and encouragement in our journey to overcome selfishness and pride.

Overcoming Selfishness and Pride

Cultivating Humility

Embracing Servanthood

Cultivating humility involves embracing a servant's heart. Jesus exemplified this in John 13:14-15: "Now that I, your Lord and Teacher, have washed your feet, you also should wash one another's feet. I have set you an example that you should do as I have done for you." Serving others shifts our focus from ourselves to meeting the needs of those around us.

Practicing Gratitude

Practicing gratitude helps counteract pride by acknowledging that all we have is a gift from God. 1 Thessalonians 5:18 encourages, "Give thanks in all circumstances; for this is God's will for you in Christ Jesus."

Gratitude fosters a humble recognition of our dependence on God and others.

Developing Empathy

Listening Actively

Developing empathy involves actively listening to others without judgment. James 1:19 advises, "My dear brothers and sisters, take note of this: Everyone should be quick to listen, slow to speak, and slow to become angry." Active listening helps us understand and connect with others' experiences and feelings.

Practicing Compassion

Compassion involves recognizing and responding to the suffering of others. Colossians 3:12 instructs, "Therefore, as God's chosen people, holy and dearly loved, clothe yourselves with compassion, kindness, humility, gentleness, and patience." Practicing compassion helps us move beyond selfishness and prioritize the well-being of others.

Embracing Vulnerability

Admitting Weaknesses

Embracing vulnerability involves admitting our weaknesses and limitations. 2 Corinthians 12:9 reminds us, "But He said to me, 'My grace is sufficient for you, for my power is made perfect in weakness.' Therefore I will boast all the more gladly about my weaknesses, so that Christ's power may rest on me." Admitting our need for God's strength fosters humility and dependence on Him.

Seeking Forgiveness

Seeking forgiveness from God and others when we recognize selfish or prideful behavior is crucial. 1 John 1:9 promises, "If we confess our sins, He is faithful and just and will forgive us our sins and purify us from all unrighteousness." Confession and repentance help restore relationships and align our hearts with God's will.

Living Out Love

Intentional Acts of Kindness

Living out love involves intentional acts of kindness. Galatians 5:13 encourages, "You, my brothers and sisters, were called to be free. But do not use your freedom to indulge the flesh; rather, serve one another humbly in love." Acts of kindness demonstrate selflessness and build a culture of love.

Building Community

Building a community involves creating an environment where love and support thrive. Acts 2:42-47 describes the early church's commitment to community and mutual care. Being part of a loving community helps us grow in love and overcome selfish and prideful tendencies.

The Role of Spiritual Disciplines

Prayer and Meditation

### Seeking God's Guidance

Prayer and meditation are essential for seeking God's guidance and strength to overcome selfishness and pride. Philippians 4:6-7 encourages, "Do not be anxious about anything, but in every situation, by prayer and petition, with thanksgiving, present your requests to God. And the peace of God, which transcends all understanding, will guard your hearts and your minds in Christ Jesus." Through prayer, we invite God to transform our hearts and align our desires with His will.

### Reflecting on Scripture

Meditating on Scripture helps renew our minds and reshape our attitudes. Romans 12:2 instructs, "Do not conform to the pattern of this world, but be transformed by the renewing of your mind. Then you will be able to test and approve what God's will is—His good, pleasing and perfect will." Reflecting on God's Word guides us in living out love and humility.

### Fasting and Self-Denial

### Cultivating Discipline

Fasting and self-denial are spiritual disciplines that help cultivate discipline and humility. Matthew 6:16-18 teaches about fasting with the right heart: "When you fast, do not look somber as the hypocrites do, for they disfigure their faces to show others they are fasting. Truly I tell you, they have received their reward in full. But when you fast, put oil on your head and wash your face, so that it will not be obvious to others that you are fasting, but only to your Father, who is unseen; and your Father, who sees what is done in secret, will reward you." These practices help us focus on God and prioritize spiritual growth over self-indulgence.

Developing Self-Control

Fasting and self-denial develop self-control, which is essential for overcoming selfish and prideful tendencies. Galatians 5:22-23 lists self-control as a fruit of the Spirit: "But the fruit of the Spirit is love, joy, peace, forbearance, kindness, goodness, faithfulness, gentleness and self-control. Against such things, there is no law."

Challenges in Overcoming Selfishness and PrideInternal Struggles

Recognizing Deep-Rooted Issues

Overcoming selfishness and pride involves addressing deep-rooted issues and tendencies. Psalm 51:10 prays, "Create in me a pure heart, O God

, and renew a steadfast spirit within me." Recognizing and confronting these issues requires honesty and openness to God's transformative work.

Persisting Despite Setbacks

The journey to overcome selfishness and pride is ongoing and may involve setbacks. Philippians 3:13-14 encourages perseverance: "Brothers and sisters, I do not consider myself yet to have taken hold of it. But one thing I do: Forgetting what is behind and straining toward what is ahead, I press on toward the goal to win the prize for which God has called me heavenward in Christ Jesus."

External Influences

Countering Cultural Norms

Cultural norms often promote selfishness and pride, making it challenging to live out Christian love and humility. Romans 12:2 calls believers to resist conforming to the world's patterns: "Do not conform to the pattern of this world, but be transformed by the renewing of your mind." Countering these influences requires intentional effort and reliance on God's guidance.

Seeking Support

Overcoming selfishness and pride is not a solitary journey. Seeking support from a community of believers provides encouragement and accountability. Hebrews 10:24-25 highlights the importance of mutual support: "And let us consider how we may spur one another on toward love and good deeds, not giving up meeting together, as some are in the habit of doing, but encouraging one another—and all the more as you see the Day approaching."

Selfishness and pride are significant barriers to loving others as Christ calls us to do. These attitudes hinder our relationships, obstruct spiritual growth, and limit God's work in our lives. By identifying and addressing these barriers through self-examination, mindfulness, humility, empathy, vulnerability, and spiritual disciplines, believers can cultivate a more loving and Christ-like life.

As we continue to explore the theology of love, let us commit to overcoming selfishness and pride, seeking God's guidance and strength in this journey. By doing so, we can build deeper, more meaningful relationships, grow spiritually, and reflect the love of Christ in all aspects of our lives. Through intentional efforts, accountability, and reliance on God's transformative work, we can overcome these barriers and live out the love that God calls us to embody.

## 6.1.0 PRACTICAL STEP FOR CULTIVATING HUMILITY AS SELFLESSNESS

Cultivating humility and selflessness is essential for overcoming the barriers of selfishness and pride, which hinder our ability to love others genuinely. This chapter explores practical steps for developing these virtues, drawing on biblical principles and practical applications. By intentionally practicing humility and selflessness, we can build deeper, more meaningful relationships and reflect the love of Christ in our lives.

Understanding Humility and Selflessness

The Nature of Humility

Recognizing Our Dependence on God

Humility involves recognizing our dependence on God and acknowledging that all we have and are comes from Him. James 4:10 states, "Humble yourselves before the Lord, and He will lift you." True humility acknowledges God's sovereignty and our need for His grace.

Valuing Others Above Ourselves

Humility also involves valuing others above ourselves. Philippians 2:3-4 encourages, "Do nothing out of selfish ambition or vain conceit. Rather, in humility value others above yourselves, not looking to your own interests but each of you to the interests of the others." This attitude fosters genuine care and respect for others.

The Nature of Selflessness

Putting Others' Needs First

Selflessness is characterized by putting others' needs and well-being before our own. Jesus exemplified this in His life and ministry. Mark 10:45 states, "For even the Son of Man did not come to be served, but to serve, and to give His life as a ransom for many." Selflessness involves a willingness to sacrifice for the benefit of others.

Acting with Compassion and Empathy

Selflessness also involves acting with compassion and empathy. Colossians 3:12 instructs, "Therefore, as God's chosen people, holy and dearly loved, clothe yourselves with compassion, kindness, humility, gentleness, and patience." These qualities enable us to connect with others and respond to their needs with genuine care.

Practical Steps for Cultivating Humility

Practicing Gratitude

Acknowledging God's Blessings

Practicing gratitude helps cultivate humility by acknowledging that all blessings come from God. 1 Thessalonians 5:18 encourages, "Give thanks in all circumstances; for this is God's will for you in Christ Jesus." Regularly expressing gratitude for God's provisions and blessings fosters a humble heart.

Expressing Thanks to Others

Expressing gratitude to others for their kindness and contributions also cultivates humility. It recognizes that we are not self-sufficient and that others play a significant role in our lives. Writing thank-you notes, offering verbal appreciation, and acknowledging others' efforts are simple yet powerful ways to practice gratitude.

Engaging in Acts of Service

Serving Without Recognition

Engaging in acts of service without seeking recognition cultivates humility. Matthew 6:3-4 teaches, "But when you give to the needy, do not let your left hand know what your right hand is doing, so that your giving may be in secret. Then your Father, who sees what is done in secret, will reward you." Serving others quietly and selflessly shifts the focus from ourselves to the needs of others.

Participating in Community Service

Participating in community service projects provides opportunities to practice humility and selflessness. Volunteering at shelters, food banks or community events helps meet the needs of others and fosters a sense of connectedness and humility.

Seeking Accountability

Inviting Feedback

Inviting feedback from trusted friends, family, or mentors helps us identify areas where we may struggle with pride or selfishness. Proverbs 27:17 states, "As iron sharpens iron, so one person sharpens another." Honest feedback and accountability help us grow in humility and selflessness.

Being Open to Correction

Being open to correction and willing to learn from others' insights is essential for cultivating humility. Proverbs 12:1 teaches, "Whoever loves discipline loves knowledge, but whoever hates correction is stupid." Embracing correction with a teachable spirit fosters personal growth and humility.

Practical Steps for Cultivating Selflessness

Practicing Active Listening

Giving Full Attention

Practicing active listening involves giving full attention to others when they speak, without interrupting or thinking about how to respond. James 1:19 advises, "My dear brothers and sisters, take note of this: Everyone should be quick to listen, slow to speak, and slow to become angry." Active listening demonstrates respect and genuine interest in others' experiences and perspectives.

Responding with Empathy

Responding with empathy involves acknowledging others' feelings and experiences. Reflecting back what you hear and expressing understanding helps build connection and shows that you care. Empathetic responses foster deeper, more meaningful relationships.

Prioritizing Others' Needs

Looking for Opportunities to Help

Prioritizing others' needs involves actively looking for opportunities to help and support those around us. Galatians 6:2 encourages, "Carry each other's burdens, and in this way you will fulfill the law of Christ." By being attentive to others' needs and offering assistance, we demonstrate selflessness and compassion.

Sacrificial Giving

Sacrificial giving involves offering our time, resources, and energy to benefit others, even when it requires personal sacrifice. 2 Corinthians 9:7 emphasizes the importance of giving with a willing heart: "Each of you should give what you have decided in your heart to give, not reluctantly or under compulsion, for God loves a cheerful giver." Sacrificial giving reflects Christ's selfless love.

Embracing Servant Leadership

Leading by Example

Servant leadership involves leading by example and prioritizing the well-being and growth of those we lead. Jesus modeled this in John 13:14-15: "Now that I, your Lord and Teacher, have washed your feet, you also should wash one another's feet. I have set you an example that you should do as I have done for you." Leading with a servant's heart fosters a culture of humility and service.

Empowering Others

Empowering others involves encouraging and equipping them to use their gifts and talents. Ephesians 4:11-12 explains, "So Christ Himself gave the apostles, the prophets, the evangelists, the pastors, and teachers, to equip His people for works of service, so that the body of Christ may be built up." By empowering others, we demonstrate selflessness and contribute to the growth of the community.

The Role of Spiritual Disciplines

Prayer and Reflection

Seeking God's Guidance

Prayer and reflection are essential for seeking God's guidance in cultivating humility and selflessness. Philippians 4:6-7 encourages, "Do not be anxious about anything, but in every situation, by prayer and petition, with thanksgiving, present your requests to God. And the peace of God, which transcends all understanding, will guard your hearts and your minds in Christ Jesus." Through prayer, we invite God to transform our hearts and guide our actions.

Reflecting on Scripture

Reflecting on Scripture helps renew our minds and align our attitudes with God's will. Romans 12:2 instructs, "Do not conform to the pattern of this world, but be transformed by the renewing of your mind. Then you will be able to test and approve what God's will is—His good, pleasing, and perfect will." Meditating on God's Word shapes our character and fosters humility and selflessness.

Fasting and Self-Denial

Cultivating Discipline

Fasting and self-denial are spiritual disciplines that help cultivate discipline and humility. Matthew 6:16-18 teaches about fasting with the right heart: "When you fast, do not look somber as the hypocrites do, for they disfigure their faces to show others they are fasting. Truly I tell you, they have received their reward in full. But when you fast, put oil on your head and wash your face, so that it will not be obvious to others that you are fasting, but only to your Father, who is unseen; and your Father, who sees what is done in secret, will reward you." These practices help us focus on God and prioritize spiritual growth over self-indulgence.

Developing Self-Control

Fasting and self-denial develop self-control, which is essential for overcoming selfish and prideful tendencies. Galatians 5:22-23 lists self-control as a fruit of the Spirit: "But the fruit of the Spirit is love, joy, peace, forbearance, kindness, goodness, faithfulness, gentleness and self-control. Against such things, there is no law."

Challenges and Opportunities

Internal Struggles

### Recognizing Deep-Rooted Issues

Overcoming selfishness and pride involves addressing deep-rooted issues and tendencies. Psalm 51:10 prays, "Create in me a pure heart, O God, and renew a steadfast spirit within me." Recognizing and confronting these issues requires honesty and openness to God's transformative work.

### Persisting Despite Setbacks

The journey to overcome selfishness and pride is ongoing and may involve setbacks. Philippians 3:13-14 encourages perseverance: "Brothers and sisters, I do not consider myself yet to have taken hold of it. But one thing I do: Forgetting what is behind and straining toward what is ahead, I press on toward the goal to win the prize for which God has called me heavenward in Christ Jesus."

### External Influences

### Countering Cultural Norms

Cultural norms often promote selfishness and pride, making it challenging to live out Christian love and humility. Romans 12:2 calls believers to resist conforming to the world's patterns: "Do not conform to the pattern of this world, but be transformed by the renewing of your mind." Countering these influences requires intentional effort and reliance on God's guidance.

### Seeking Support

Overcoming selfishness and pride is not a solitary journey. Seeking support from a community of believers provides encouragement and accountability. Hebrews 10:24-25 highlights the importance of mutual support: "And let us consider how we may spur one another on toward love and good deeds, not giving up meeting together, as some are in the habit of doing, but encouraging one another—and all the more as you see the Day approaching."

Cultivating humility and selflessness is essential for overcoming the barriers of selfishness and pride, which hinder our ability to love others genuinely. By practicing gratitude, engaging in acts of service, seeking accountability, practicing active listening, prioritizing others' needs, embracing servant leadership, and engaging in spiritual disciplines, believers can develop these virtues and reflect the love of Christ in their lives.

As we continue to explore the theology of love, let us commit to cultivating humility and selflessness, seeking God's guidance and strength in this journey. By doing so, we can build deeper, more meaningful relationships, grow spiritually, and reflect the love of Christ in all aspects of our lives. Through intentional efforts, accountability, and reliance on God's transformative work, we can overcome these barriers and live out the love that God calls us to embody.

# 6.2.0 LOVING IN THE MIDST OF SUFFERING

Loving others in the midst of suffering presents one of the most profound challenges to living out the Christian faith. Pain and loss can make it difficult to maintain a posture of love, both towards others and even towards God. This chapter explores the nature of suffering, the biblical call to love amidst hardship, and practical steps to sustain love during times of pain and loss.

Understanding Suffering

The Reality of Suffering

Universal Experience

Suffering is a universal human experience. Jesus acknowledged this reality in John 16:33, saying, "In this world, you will have trouble. But take heart! I have overcome the world." Everyone faces trials and hardships, whether through personal loss, illness, broken relationships, or other forms of pain.

Spiritual and Emotional Impact

Suffering affects us not only physically but also emotionally and spiritually. It can lead to feelings of despair, anger, and doubt. The psalmists frequently expressed these feelings, as in Psalm 13:1-2: "How long, Lord? Will you forget

241

me forever? How long will you hide your face from me? How long must I wrestle with my thoughts and day after day have sorrow in my heart?"

The Purpose of Suffering

Growth and Refinement

The Bible teaches that suffering can have a purpose in God's plan, often leading to spiritual growth and refinement. Romans 5:3-5 explains, "Not only so, but we also glory in our sufferings because we know that suffering produces perseverance; perseverance, character; and character, hope. And hope does not put us to shame, because God's love has been poured out into our hearts through the Holy Spirit, who has been given to us."

Sharing in Christ's Sufferings

Suffering also allows believers to share in Christ's sufferings, deepening their connection with Him. Philippians 3:10-11 expresses this desire: "I want to know Christ—yes, to know the power of His resurrection and participation in His sufferings, becoming like Him in His death, and so, somehow, attaining to the resurrection from the dead."

Biblical Call to Love Amidst Suffering

Jesus' Example

Unconditional Love

Jesus exemplified unconditional love in the midst of His own suffering. On the cross, He prayed for those who crucified Him, saying, "Father, forgive them, for they do not know what they are doing" (Luke 23:34). His love extended even to His enemies, setting a profound example for us to follow.

Sacrificial Love

Jesus' sacrificial love is a model for how we are to love others, even in the face of suffering. John 15:13 teaches, "Greater love has no one than this: to lay down one's life for one's friends." His willingness to endure the cross for our sake challenges us to love selflessly, even when it is difficult.

Paul's Teachings

Love in Hardship

The Apostle Paul frequently wrote about maintaining love in the midst of suffering. In Romans 12:12-13, he instructs, "Be joyful in hope, patient in affliction, faithful in prayer. Share with the Lord's people who are in need. Practice hospitality." Paul's letters often emphasize the importance of continuing to love and serve others, regardless of personal trials.

Endurance and Encouragement

Paul also encouraged believers to endure and support one another through suffering. In Galatians 6:2, he writes,

"Carry each other's burdens, and in this way, you will fulfill the law of Christ." Loving others involves bearing their burdens and providing encouragement during difficult times.

Practical Steps for Loving in the Midst of Suffering

Maintaining a Relationship with God

Prayer and Lament

Maintaining an open and honest relationship with God is crucial during times of suffering. The Bible encourages bringing our pain and questions to God through prayer and lament. Psalm 62:8 advises, "Trust in Him at all times, you people; pour out your hearts to Him, for God is our refuge." Expressing our feelings to God can provide comfort and strength.

Seeking God's Presence

Seeking God's presence through worship and meditation on Scripture helps sustain love during hardship. Psalm 34:18 assures, "The Lord is close to the brokenhearted and saves those who are crushed in spirit." Drawing near to God in times of pain can renew our spirit and empower us to continue loving others.

Practicing Self-Care

Physical and Emotional Health

Taking care of our physical and emotional health is essential for maintaining the capacity to love others. Ensuring adequate rest, nutrition, and exercise, as well as seeking professional help when needed, allows us to remain resilient. 1 Corinthians 6:19-20 reminds us that our bodies are temples of the Holy Spirit and should be cared for accordingly.

Setting Boundaries

Setting healthy boundaries is important to prevent burnout and ensure we have the energy to love others. Jesus Himself took time to rest and withdraw from the crowds to pray (Mark 1:35). Following His example, we should balance caring for others with taking time to replenish our own well-being.

Finding Support

Community and Fellowship

Engaging with a supportive community can provide strength and encouragement during times of suffering. Hebrews 10:24-25 emphasizes the importance of fellowship: "And let us consider how we may spur one another on toward love and good deeds, not giving up meeting together, as some are in the habit of doing, but encouraging one another—and all the more as you see the Day approaching." Being part of a church or small group offers a network of support.

Counseling and Therapy

Seeking counseling or therapy can be a vital resource for processing pain and loss. Proverbs 11:14 highlights the value of wise counsel: "For lack of guidance a nation falls, but victory is won through many advisers." Professional help can provide strategies for coping and maintaining emotional health.

Serving Others

Acts of Kindness

Engaging in acts of kindness, even when we are suffering, can shift our focus from our own pain to the needs of others. Acts 20:35 recalls Jesus' teaching, "It is more blessed to give than to receive." Serving others can provide a sense of purpose and fulfillment, even in difficult times.

Volunteering

Volunteering in community service or ministry can also be a powerful way to continue loving others amidst suffering. Whether it's through food drives, visiting the sick, or mentoring, these acts of service embody the love of Christ and can be healing for both the giver and the recipient.

Cultivating Hope and Resilience

Faith and Hope in God's Promises

Cultivating hope and resilience involves anchoring our faith in God's promises. Romans 8:28 offers assurance, "And we know that in all things God works for the good of those who love Him, who have been called according to His purpose." Trusting in God's sovereign plan helps sustain love and hope during suffering.

Developing a Resilient Mindset

Developing a resilient mindset involves focusing on growth and learning through hardship. James 1:2-4 encourages, "Consider it pure joy, my brothers and sisters, whenever you face trials of many kinds, because you know that the testing of your faith produces perseverance. Let perseverance finish its work so that you may be mature and complete, not lacking anything." Viewing suffering as an opportunity for growth fosters resilience and a deeper capacity to love.

The Role of Love in Healing and Transformation

Personal Healing

Healing Through Love

Loving others can be a pathway to personal healing. Acts of kindness and compassion can provide a sense of purpose and joy, even in the midst of pain. Proverbs 11:25 states, "A generous person will prosper; whoever refreshes others will be refreshed." Loving others can bring refreshment and healing to our own hearts.

Transforming Pain into Purpose

Transforming pain into purpose involves using our experiences of suffering to empathize with and support others. 2 Corinthians 1:3-4 describes God's comfort in our trials: "Praise be to the God and Father of our Lord Jesus Christ, the Father of compassion and the God of all comfort, who comforts us in all our troubles so that we can comfort those in any trouble with the comfort we ourselves receive from God." Our experiences can equip us to minister to others in their suffering.

Community Healing

Building Stronger Bonds

Suffering can strengthen community bonds as people come together to support one another. Galatians 6:2 urges, "Carry each other's burdens, and in this way you will fulfill the law of Christ." Shared experiences of suffering and support can create deeper connections and a more compassionate community.

Fostering a Culture of Compassion

Fostering a culture of compassion within the community involves encouraging empathy and support for those who are suffering. Colossians 3:12 calls believers to "clothe yourselves with compassion, kindness, humility, gentleness and patience." A compassionate community reflects the love of Christ and provides a safe haven for those in pain.

Loving in the midst of suffering is a profound challenge, yet it is also a powerful testament to the transformative power of Christ's love. By understanding the nature and purpose of suffering, maintaining a relationship with God, practicing self-care, finding support, serving others, and cultivating hope and resilience, believers can sustain love even in the hardest times.

As we continue to explore the theology of love, let us commit to loving others faithfully, even in the midst of our own suffering. By doing so, we reflect the heart of Christ, build deeper relationships, and foster a compassionate community that honors God and supports one another through life's trials. Through intentional practices, reliance on God's strength, and a commitment to love, we can overcome the challenges of suffering and continue to embody the love that God calls us to live out.

## 6.2.1 FINDING STRENGTH IN GOD'S LOVE DURING DIFFICULT TIMES

During the most challenging times of our lives, finding strength in God's love can provide the comfort, courage, and resilience needed to persevere. This chapter explores how to draw strength from God's love, examining biblical foundations, practical steps, and personal testimonies that illustrate the power of God's love to sustain us in hardship.

Biblical Foundations for Finding Strength in God's Love

God's Unfailing Love

Ever-Present Help

God's love is a constant and unfailing source of strength. Psalm 46:1-2 declares, "God is our refuge and strength, an ever-present help in trouble. Therefore we will not fear, though the earth give way and the mountains fall into the heart of the sea." Recognizing God as our refuge helps us find peace and stability amidst chaos.

Unconditional Love

Romans 8:38-39 assures us of God's unwavering love: "For I am convinced that neither death nor life, neither angels nor demons, neither the present nor the future, nor any powers, neither height nor depth nor anything else in all creation, will be able to separate us from the love of God that is in Christ Jesus our Lord." This passage reminds us that God's love is unconditional and unbreakable, providing a secure foundation during difficult times.

Strength in Weakness

Paul's Testimony

The Apostle Paul experienced immense suffering yet found strength in God's love. In 2 Corinthians 12:9-10, Paul recounts God's words to him: "But He said to me, 'My grace is sufficient for you, for my power is made perfect in weakness.' Therefore I will boast all the more gladly about my weaknesses, so that Christ's power may rest on me. That is why, for Christ's sake, I delight in weaknesses, in insults, in hardships, in persecutions, in difficulties. For when I am weak, then I am strong." Paul's testimony shows that God's love and grace are most powerful when we are at our weakest.

God's Faithfulness

Lamentations' Assurance

In Lamentations 3:22-23, the prophet Jeremiah finds hope in God's faithfulness despite profound suffering: "Because of the Lord's great love we are not consumed, for His compassions never fail. They are new every morning; great is Your faithfulness." This assurance of God's constant compassion and faithfulness provides hope and strength.

Practical Steps for Finding Strength in God's Love

Seeking God in Prayer

Pouring Out Our Hearts

Prayer is a vital practice for finding strength in God's love. Psalm 62:8 encourages us, "Trust in Him at all times, you people; pour out your hearts to Him, for God is our refuge."

By bringing our fears, doubts, and pain to God in prayer, we can experience His comforting presence and gain the strength to endure.

Listening to God's Voice

Prayer is not only about speaking to God but also about listening to His voice. Spending time in quiet reflection and meditation allows us to hear God's reassurances and guidance, deepening our sense of His love and presence.

Immersing in Scripture

Finding Promises

Scripture is filled with promises of God's love and faithfulness. Meditating on these promises can provide immense strength during difficult times. Joshua 1:9 offers encouragement: "Have I not commanded you? Be strong and courageous. Do not be afraid; do not be discouraged, for the Lord your God will be with you wherever you go." Reflecting on God's promises helps us anchor our hope and trust in Him.

Learning from Biblical Examples

Studying the lives of biblical figures who endured suffering can provide insights and inspiration. Job, Joseph, David, and Paul all faced significant hardships yet remained steadfast in their faith. Their stories illustrate how reliance on God's love can lead to perseverance and victory.

Worship and Praise

Expressing Gratitude

Worship and praise shift our focus from our problems to God's greatness and love. Psalm 103:1-2 exhorts, "Praise the Lord, my soul; all my inmost being, praise His holy name. Praise the Lord, my soul, and forget not all His benefits." Expressing gratitude for God's blessings and faithfulness can uplift our spirits and strengthen our resolve.

Rejoicing in God's Goodness

Even in difficult times, rejoicing in God's goodness can transform our perspective. Philippians 4:4 encourages, "Rejoice in the Lord always. I will say it again: Rejoice!" Celebrating God's goodness and love helps us maintain a positive outlook and find strength.

Connecting with Community

Supportive Relationships

Building and maintaining supportive relationships within a faith community provides strength and encouragement. Hebrews 10:24-25 emphasizes the importance of fellowship: "And let us consider how we may spur one another on toward love and good deeds, not giving up meeting together, as some are in the habit of doing, but encouraging one another—and all the more as you see the

Day approaching." Engaging with others who share our faith helps us draw strength from collective support.

Sharing Burdens

Galatians 6:2 instructs, "Carry each other's burdens, and in this way you will fulfill the law of Christ." Sharing our struggles with trusted friends, mentors, or small groups can lighten our load and provide practical and emotional support.

Serving Others

Acts of Kindness

Serving others, even when we are struggling, can provide a sense of purpose and fulfillment. Acts 20:35 recalls Jesus' teaching, "It is more blessed to give than to receive." Acts of kindness and service can shift our focus from our own pain to the needs of others, bringing joy and strength.

Volunteering

Volunteering in community service or church ministries allows us to live out God's love and find strength through meaningful engagement. Whether it's helping at a food bank, mentoring, or visiting the sick, these acts of service embody Christ's love and provide a sense of connection and purpose.

Personal Testimonies of Strength in God's Love

Stories of Faith

Job's Perseverance

The story of Job is a profound example of finding strength in God's love during immense suffering. Despite losing his family, wealth, and health, Job remained faithful to God. Job 1:21 reflects his trust: "The Lord gave and the Lord has taken away; may the name of the Lord be praised." Job's perseverance and ultimate restoration highlight the sustaining power of God's love.

Corrie ten Boom's Forgiveness

Corrie ten Boom, a survivor of the Holocaust, found strength in God's love to forgive those who persecuted her. Her story, documented in "The Hiding Place," illustrates how God's love can enable forgiveness and healing even in the face of unimaginable suffering.

Modern-Day Examples

Testimonies of Healing

Many modern believers have shared testimonies of finding strength in God's love during illness, loss, and other trials. These stories often highlight how prayer, scripture, community support, and acts of service have provided resilience and hope.

Inspiration for Others

Sharing personal testimonies of God's love and faithfulness can inspire and encourage others facing similar struggles. Hearing how others have drawn strength from

God's love helps build faith and provides a sense of shared experience and support.

Challenges and Opportunities

Overcoming Doubt and Fear

Trusting God's Plan

Doubt and fear are natural responses to suffering, but they can be overcome by trusting in God's plan. Proverbs 3:5-6 advises, "Trust in the Lord with all your heart and lean not on your own understanding; in all your ways submit to Him, and He will make your paths straight." Trusting that God has a purpose for our pain helps us find strength and hope.

Embracing God's Sovereignty

Embracing God's sovereignty means acknowledging that He is in control, even when circumstances seem overwhelming. Isaiah 55:8-9 reminds us, "For my thoughts are not your thoughts, neither are your ways my ways," declares the Lord. "As the heavens are higher than the earth, so are my ways higher than your ways and my thoughts than your thoughts." Trusting in God's wisdom and love helps us navigate our struggles with faith.

Navigating Grief and Loss

Allowing Yourself to Grieve

Finding strength in God's love doesn't mean ignoring or suppressing our grief. Ecclesiastes 3:4 acknowledges, "A time to weep and a time to laugh, a time to mourn and a time to dance." Allowing ourselves to grieve and process our emotions is a healthy part of healing.

Finding Hope in God's Promises

Even in the midst of grief, finding hope in God's promises provides comfort. Revelation 21:4 offers a vision of the future: "He will wipe every tear from their eyes. There will be no more death or mourning or crying or pain, for the old order of things has passed away." This promise of eternal life and restoration gives us hope beyond our current suffering.

Finding strength in God's love during difficult times is a profound and transformative experience. By seeking God in prayer, immersing ourselves in Scripture, engaging in worship and praise, connecting with the community, serving others, and learning from personal testimonies, we can draw on the sustaining power of God's love to navigate our struggles.

As we continue to explore the theology of love, let us commit to finding and drawing strength from God's love, trusting in His faithfulness and sovereignty. By doing so, we can face our challenges with resilience and hope, reflecting the love of Christ in our lives and inspiring others with our testimony of God's enduring love and grace. Through intentional practices, reliance on God's strength, and a commitment to love, we can overcome the challenges of suffering and continue to embody the love that God calls us to live out.

## 6.3.0 FORGIVENESS AND RECONCILIATION

Forgiveness and reconciliation are central to the Christian faith and are vital for maintaining healthy relationships and a loving community. Love plays a crucial role in the process of forgiveness, enabling us to let go of past hurts and rebuild trust. This chapter explores the biblical foundations of forgiveness and reconciliation, the importance of love in these processes, and practical steps to achieve genuine forgiveness and reconciliation.

Biblical Foundations for Forgiveness and Reconciliation

God's Forgiveness

Unconditional Forgiveness

God's forgiveness is a cornerstone of the Christian faith. Ephesians 1:7 declares, "In Him we have redemption through His blood, the forgiveness of sins, in accordance with the riches of God's grace." God's unconditional forgiveness through Jesus Christ sets the example for us to forgive others.

Forgiving as We Have Been Forgiven

Jesus emphasizes the importance of forgiving others as we have been forgiven by God. In Matthew 6:14-15, He teaches, "For if you forgive other people when they sin against you, your heavenly Father will also forgive you. But if you do not forgive others their sins, your Father will not forgive your sins." This reciprocal relationship underscores the necessity of forgiveness in our lives.

Jesus' Teachings on Forgiveness

The Parable of the Unforgiving Servant

In Matthew 18:21-35, Jesus tells the Parable of the Unforgiving Servant to illustrate the importance of forgiveness. The parable concludes with a stern warning: "This is how my heavenly Father will treat each of you unless you forgive your brother or sister from your heart." This parable emphasizes that forgiving others is not optional but a vital part of our faith.

Seventy Times Seven

When Peter asked Jesus how many times he should forgive someone who sins against him, Jesus responded, "I tell you, not seven times, but seventy-seven times" (Matthew 18:22). This response highlights that forgiveness should be limitless and continuous, reflecting God's boundless grace.

Reconciliation in the Early Church

Paul's Teachings on Reconciliation

The Apostle Paul emphasizes the importance of reconciliation in the church. In 2 Corinthians 5:18-19, he writes, "All this is from God, who reconciled us to Himself through Christ and gave us the ministry of reconciliation: that God was reconciling the world to Himself in Christ, not counting people's sins against them. And He has committed to us the message of reconciliation." Paul teaches that believers are called to be agents of reconciliation, mirroring God's work in Christ.

Healing Broken Relationships

Paul also addresses the need for reconciliation in personal relationships. In Ephesians 4:32, he instructs, "Be kind and compassionate to one another, forgiving each other, just as in Christ God forgave you." This call to kindness, compassion, and forgiveness fosters healing and unity within the church.

The Role of Love in Forgiveness and Reconciliation

Love as the Foundation of Forgiveness

Agape Love

Agape love, the selfless and unconditional love of God, is the foundation of forgiveness. 1 Corinthians 13:4-7 describes the nature of agape love: "Love is patient, love is kind. It does not envy, it does not boast, it is not proud. It does not dishonor others, it is not self-seeking, it is not easily angered, and it keeps no record of wrongs. Love does not delight in evil but rejoices with the truth. It always protects, always trusts, always hopes, always perseveres." This love enables us to forgive others, even when it is difficult.

Forgiving from the Heart

True forgiveness comes from the heart, motivated by love. Colossians 3:13 advises, "Bear with each other and forgive one another if any of you has a grievance against someone. Forgive as the Lord forgave you." Love helps us to let go of grudges and resentment, allowing genuine forgiveness to take place.

Love as the Catalyst for Reconciliation

Healing Wounds

Love is the catalyst for reconciliation, helping to heal wounds and restore relationships. Proverbs 10:12 states, "Hatred stirs up conflict, but love covers over all wrongs." Love seeks to mend what is broken and bring peace where there is conflict.

Building Trust

Reconciliation involves rebuilding trust, and love is essential in this process. 1 Peter 4:8 encourages, "Above all, love each other deeply because love covers over a multitude of sins." Deep, genuine love fosters an environment where trust can be rebuilt and relationships can flourish.

Practical Steps for Forgiveness

Acknowledging the Hurt

Facing the Pain

The first step in forgiveness is acknowledging the hurt and facing the pain it has caused. Psalm 34:18 offers comfort: "The Lord is close to the brokenhearted and saves those who are crushed in spirit." Recognizing the impact of the offense is essential for the healing process.

Validating Feelings

Validating our feelings and those of others involved helps in understanding the depth of the hurt. Romans 12:15 advises, "Rejoice with those who rejoice; mourn with those who mourn." Empathy and compassion facilitate the journey towards forgiveness.

Choosing to Forgive

Making the Decision

Forgiveness is a choice, not a feeling. It involves deciding to let go of the desire for revenge and to release the offender from the debt owed. Mark 11:25 instructs, "And when you stand praying, if you hold anything against anyone, forgive them, so that your Father in heaven may forgive you your sins." This decision aligns us with God's command to forgive.

Seeking God's Help

Forgiveness can be challenging, and seeking God's help through prayer is vital. Philippians 4:13 reminds us, "I can do all this through Him who gives me strength." Relying on God's strength enables us to forgive even when it seems impossible.

Extending Grace

Offering Forgiveness

Extending grace to others involves offering forgiveness freely, as God has forgiven us. Ephesians 4:32 calls us to "Be kind and compassionate to one another, forgiving each other, just as in Christ God forgave you." This grace reflects God's love and mercy.

Letting Go of Resentment

Letting go of resentment is crucial for true forgiveness. Hebrews 12:15 warns, "See to it that no one falls short of the grace of God and that no bitter root grows up to cause trouble and defile many." Releasing bitterness allows healing and peace to take root.

Practical Steps for Reconciliation

Initiating Reconciliation

Taking the First Step

Reconciliation often requires someone to take the first step. Matthew 5:23-24 advises, "Therefore if you are offering your gift at the altar and there remember that your brother or sister has something against you, leave your gift there in front of the altar. First, go and be reconciled to them; then come and offer your gift." Initiating reconciliation demonstrates a commitment to restoring the relationship.

Seeking Mediation

In some cases, seeking mediation from a neutral third party can help facilitate reconciliation. Matthew 18:15-17 outlines this process: "If your brother or sister sins, go and point out their fault, just between the two of you. If they listen to you, you have won them over. But if they will not listen, take one or two others along, so that 'every matter may be established by the testimony of two or three witnesses.' If they still refuse to listen, tell it to the church."

Communicating Effectively

Open and Honest Dialogue

Effective communication is essential for reconciliation. Ephesians 4:15 encourages, "Instead, speaking the truth in love, we will grow to become in every respect the mature body of Him who is the head, that is, Christ." Open and honest dialogue helps address misunderstandings and fosters mutual understanding.

Active Listening

Active listening involves giving full attention to the other person and acknowledging their perspective. James 1:19

advises, "My dear brothers and sisters, take note of this: Everyone should be quick to listen, slow to speak, and slow to become angry." Listening well is key to resolving conflicts and rebuilding relationships.

Restoring Trust

Consistency and Integrity

Restoring trust takes time and requires consistency and integrity. Proverbs 12:22 states, "The Lord detests lying lips, but He delights in people who are trustworthy." Demonstrating reliability and honesty helps rebuild trust.

Setting Boundaries

Setting healthy boundaries can protect the relationship and ensure mutual respect. Boundaries help prevent further harm and create a safe space for the relationship to heal and grow.

The Challenges of Forgiveness and Reconciliation

Overcoming Pride and Fear

Humility and Courage

Forgiveness and reconciliation often require overcoming pride and fear. Philippians 2:3-4 encourages, "Do nothing out of selfish ambition or vain conceit. Rather, in humility value others above yourselves, not looking to your own interests but each of you to the interests of the others."

Humility and courage are essential for taking the steps toward forgiveness and reconciliation.

Trusting God's Plan

Trusting in God's plan and timing is crucial. Romans 8:28 reassures us, "And we know that in all things God works for the good of those who love Him, who have been called according to His purpose." Trusting that God can bring good out of difficult situations helps us to forgive and seek reconciliation.

Dealing with Unrepentance

Forgiving Without Reconciliation

In some cases, the other party may be unrepentant or unwilling to reconcile. Even in these situations, we are called to forgive. Romans 12:18 advises, "If it is possible, as far as

it depends on you, live at peace with everyone." Forgiving without reconciliation frees us from bitterness, even if the relationship cannot be fully restored.

Finding Peace in God's Love

Finding peace in God's love and trusting Him with the outcome allows us to move forward. Philippians 4:7 promises, "And the peace of God, which transcends all understanding, will guard your hearts and your minds in Christ Jesus." God's peace sustains us when reconciliation is not possible.

Forgiveness and reconciliation are integral to living out the Christian faith and maintaining healthy, loving relationships. Love plays a crucial role in these processes, enabling us to let go of past hurts and rebuild trust. By understanding the biblical foundations of forgiveness and reconciliation, embracing the role of love, and following practical steps, we can achieve genuine forgiveness and reconciliation.

As we continue to explore the theology of love, let us commit to forgiving others as God has forgiven us and seeking reconciliation where possible. By doing so, we reflect the heart of Christ and build a community characterized by love, healing, and unity. Through intentional practices, reliance on God's strength, and a commitment to love, we can overcome the challenges of forgiveness and reconciliation and live out the love that God calls us to embody.

## 6.3.1 RECONCILIATION AS AN EXPRESSION OF DIVINE LOVE

Reconciliation is a profound expression of divine love, mirroring God's own actions toward humanity. It involves restoring broken relationships and healing the wounds of division. This chapter explores the theological foundations of reconciliation, the role of divine love in this process, and practical steps to foster reconciliation in our personal lives and communities.

Theological Foundations of Reconciliation

God's Act of Reconciliation

Reconciliation through Christ

God initiated the ultimate act of reconciliation through Jesus Christ. 2 Corinthians 5:18-19 declares, "All this is from God, who reconciled us to Himself through Christ and gave us the ministry of reconciliation: that God was reconciling the world to Himself in Christ, not counting people's sins against them. And He has committed to us the message of reconciliation." Through Christ's sacrificial death and resurrection, God restored the broken relationship between Himself and humanity.

Forgiveness as the Basis

Forgiveness is the foundation of reconciliation. Colossians 1:21-22 explains, "Once you were alienated from God and were enemies in your minds because of your evil behavior. But now He has reconciled you by Christ's physical body through death to present you holy in His sight, without blemish and free from accusation." God's forgiveness, extended through Christ, makes reconciliation possible.

Jesus' Teachings on Reconciliation

The Sermon on the Mount

Jesus emphasized the importance of reconciliation in His teachings. In Matthew 5:23-24, He states, "Therefore, if you are offering your gift at the altar and there remember that your brother or sister has something against you, leave your gift there in front of the altar. First, go and be reconciled to them; then come and offer your gift." This instruction highlights the priority of reconciling relationships over religious rituals.

Loving Enemies

In Matthew 5:43-45, Jesus further teaches, "You have heard that it was said, 'Love your neighbor and hate your enemy.' But I tell you, love your enemies and pray for those who persecute you, that you may be children of your Father in heaven." Loving our enemies and seeking reconciliation with them reflects the divine love that God shows to all people.

Paul's Teachings on Reconciliation

Unity in the Body of Christ

The Apostle Paul emphasized the importance of unity and reconciliation within the church. Ephesians 4:3-6 urges believers to "Make every effort to keep the unity of the Spirit through the bond of peace. There is one body and one Spirit, just as you were called to one hope when you were called; one Lord, one faith, one baptism; one God and Father of all, who is over all and through all and in all." Reconciliation promotes unity and reflects the oneness of the body of Christ.

Ministry of Reconciliation

Paul also called believers to participate in the ministry of reconciliation. In 2 Corinthians 5:20, he writes, "We are therefore Christ's ambassadors, as though God were making His appeal through us. We implore you on Christ's behalf: Be reconciled to God." As ambassadors of Christ, believers are called to embody and promote reconciliation.

The Role of Divine Love in Reconciliation

Agape Love as the Foundation

Selfless and Unconditional Love

Agape love, the selfless and unconditional love of God, is the foundation of reconciliation. 1 Corinthians 13:4-7 describes this love: "Love is patient, love is kind. It does not envy, it does not boast, it is not proud. It does not dishonor others, it is not self-seeking, it is not easily angered, it keeps no record of wrongs. Love does not delight in evil but rejoices with the truth. It always protects, always trusts, always hopes, always perseveres." This divine love empowers us to seek reconciliation, even when it is difficult.

Forgiving as God Forgives

Divine love enables us to forgive others as God has forgiven us. Colossians 3:13 instructs, "Bear with each other and forgive one another if any of you has a grievance against someone. Forgive as the Lord forgave you." Forgiveness motivated by divine love paves the way for reconciliation.

Healing and Restoration

Mending Broken Relationships

Reconciliation involves the healing and restoration of broken relationships. Proverbs 10:12 states, "Hatred stirs up conflict, but love covers over all wrongs." Divine love seeks to mend what is broken and bring peace where there is conflict.

Building Bridges

Divine love helps build bridges between divided individuals and communities. Ephesians 2:14-16 emphasizes that Christ has broken down the dividing wall of hostility: "For He Himself is our peace, who has made the two groups one and has destroyed the barrier, the dividing wall of hostility, by setting aside in His flesh the law with its commands and regulations. His purpose was to create in Himself one new humanity out of the two, thus making peace, and in one body to reconcile both of them to God through the cross, by which He put to death their hostility." Love-driven reconciliation fosters unity and peace.

Practical Steps for Fostering Reconciliation

Acknowledging the Need for Reconciliation

Recognizing Brokenness

The first step in reconciliation is acknowledging the brokenness in our relationships. Romans 12:18 advises, "If it is possible, as far as it depends on you, live at peace with everyone." Recognizing where reconciliation is needed allows us to take intentional steps toward healing.

Confession and Repentance

Confession and repentance are crucial for reconciliation. James 5:16 encourages, "Therefore confess your sins to each other and pray for each other so that you may be healed. The prayer of a righteous person is powerful and effective." Admitting our wrongs and seeking forgiveness opens the door to reconciliation.

Initiating Reconciliation

Taking the First Step

Reconciliation often requires someone to take the first step. Matthew 5:23-24 advises, "Therefore if you are offering your gift at the altar and there remember that your brother or sister has something against you, leave your gift there in front of the altar. First, go and be reconciled to them; then come and offer your gift." Initiating reconciliation demonstrates a commitment to restoring the relationship.

Seeking Mediation

In some cases, seeking mediation from a neutral third party can help facilitate reconciliation. Matthew 18:15-17 outlines this process: "If your brother or sister sins, go and point out their fault, just between the two of you. If they listen to you, you have won them over. But if they will not listen, take one or two others along, so that 'every matter may be established by the testimony of two or three witnesses.' If they still refuse to listen, tell it to the church."

Communicating Effectively

Open and Honest Dialogue

Effective communication is essential for reconciliation. Ephesians 4:15 encourages, "Instead, speaking the truth in love, we will grow to become in every respect the mature body of Him who is the head, that is, Christ." Open and honest dialogue helps address misunderstandings and fosters mutual understanding.

Active Listening

Active listening involves giving full attention to the other person and acknowledging their perspective. James 1:19 advises, "My dear brothers and sisters, take note of this: Everyone should be quick to listen, slow to speak, and slow to become angry." Listening well is key to resolving conflicts and rebuilding relationships.

Extending Forgiveness

Offering Forgiveness Freely

Extending forgiveness freely, as God has forgiven us, is vital for reconciliation. Ephesians 4:32 calls us to "Be kind and compassionate to one another, forgiving each other, just as in Christ God forgave you." This grace reflects God's love and mercy.

Letting Go of Resentment

Letting go of resentment is crucial for true reconciliation. Hebrews 12:15 warns, "See to it that no one falls short of the grace of God and that no bitter root grows up to cause trouble and defile many." Releasing bitterness allows healing and peace to take root.

Restoring Trust

Consistency and Integrity

Restoring trust takes time and requires consistency and integrity. Proverbs 12:22 states, "The Lord detests lying lips, but He delights in people who are trustworthy." Demonstrating reliability and honesty helps rebuild trust.

Setting Boundaries

Setting healthy boundaries can protect the relationship and ensure mutual respect. Boundaries help prevent further harm and create a safe space for the relationship to heal and grow.

The Impact of Reconciliation

Personal Healing

Emotional and Spiritual Well-being

Reconciliation promotes emotional and spiritual well-being by freeing individuals from the burden of unresolved conflict. Matthew 11:28-30 invites us to find rest in Jesus: "Come to me, all you who are weary and burdened, and I will give you rest. Take my yoke upon you and learn from me, for I am gentle and humble in heart, and you will find rest for your souls. For my yoke is easy and my burden is light." Reconciliation brings peace and healing to our hearts.

Growth in Love and Compassion

Reconciliation fosters growth in love and compassion, reflecting the character of Christ. Colossians 3:14 advises, "And over all these virtues put on love, which binds them all together in perfect unity." As we practice reconciliation, we grow in our ability to love others deeply and selflessly.

Community Strengthening

Building a Culture of Peace

Reconciliation strengthens the community by building a culture of peace and unity. Ephesians 4:3 encourages, "Make every effort to keep the unity of the

Spirit through the bond of peace." A reconciled community reflects the love and harmony of God's Kingdom.

Fostering Mutual Support

Reconciled relationships foster mutual support and encouragement. Galatians 6:2 instructs, "Carry each other's burdens, and in this way, you will fulfill the law of Christ." A supportive community provides a strong foundation for individuals to thrive.

Challenges in Reconciliation

Overcoming Pride and Fear

Humility and Courage

Reconciliation often requires overcoming pride and fear. Philippians 2:3-4 encourages, "Do nothing out of selfish ambition or vain conceit. Rather, in humility value others above yourselves, not looking to your own interests but each of you to the interests of the others." Humility and courage are essential for taking the steps toward reconciliation.

Trusting God's Plan

Trusting in God's plan and timing is crucial. Romans 8:28 reassures us, "And we know that in all things God works for the good of those who love Him, who have been called according to His purpose." Trusting that God can bring good out of difficult situations helps us to seek reconciliation.

Dealing with Unrepentance

Forgiving Without Reconciliation

In some cases, the other party may be unrepentant or unwilling to reconcile. Even in these situations, we are called to forgive. Romans 12:18 advises, "If it is possible, as far as it depends on you, live at peace with everyone." Forgiving without reconciliation frees us from bitterness, even if the relationship cannot be fully restored.

Finding Peace in God's Love

Finding peace in God's love and trusting Him with the outcome allows us to move forward. Philippians 4:7 promises, "And the peace of God, which transcends all understanding, will guard your hearts and your minds in Christ Jesus." God's peace sustains us when reconciliation is not possible.

Reconciliation is a profound expression of divine love, mirroring God's actions toward humanity through Jesus Christ. By understanding the theological foundations of reconciliation, embracing the role of divine love, and following practical steps, we can foster genuine reconciliation in our personal lives and communities.

As we continue to explore the theology of love, let us commit to being agents of reconciliation, reflecting the heart of Christ in our relationships. Through intentional practices, reliance on God's strength, and a commitment to love, we can overcome the challenges of reconciliation and embody the love that God calls us to live out. By doing so, we contribute to building a community characterized by peace, unity, and mutual support, reflecting the Kingdom of God on earth.

CHAPTER 07

---

## THE ESCHATOLOGY OF LOVE
### 7.1. The Fulfillment of Love in the Kingdom of God

The concept of eschatology, the study of the end times and the final destiny of humanity is profoundly intertwined with the theology of love. The future hope of perfect love in God's Kingdom is a central theme in Christian eschatology. This chapter explores the biblical foundations of eschatological love, the promise of its fulfillment in God's Kingdom, and the implications for our lives today.

Biblical Foundations of Eschatological Love

The Promise of God's Kingdom

A New Heaven and a New Earth

The Bible promises a future where God's perfect love will be fully realized. Revelation 21:1-4 describes this hope: "Then I saw 'a new heaven and a new earth,' for the first heaven and the first earth had passed away, and there was no longer any sea. I saw the Holy City, the new Jerusalem, coming down out of heaven from God, prepared as a bride beautifully dressed for her husband. And I heard a loud voice from the throne saying, 'Look! God's dwelling place is now among the people, and He will dwell with them. They will be His people, and God Himself will be with them and be their God. He will wipe every tear from their eyes. There will be no more death or mourning or crying or pain, for the old order of things has passed away.'" This vision of a new creation reflects the ultimate fulfillment of God's love.

The Marriage Supper of the Lamb

Revelation 19:7-9 speaks of the marriage supper of the Lamb, symbolizing the union between Christ and His church: "Let us rejoice and be glad and give Him glory! For the wedding of the Lamb has come, and His bride has made herself ready. Fine linen, bright and clean, was given her to wear. (Fine linen stands for the righteous acts of God's holy people.) Then the angel said to me, 'Write this: Blessed are those who are invited to the wedding supper of the Lamb!' And he added, 'These are the true words of God.'" This event represents the consummation of divine love and the eternal relationship between Christ and His followers.

The Restoration of All Things

The Prophetic Vision

The prophetic books of the Old Testament often speak of a future restoration marked by peace, justice, and divine love. Isaiah 65:17-25 presents a vision of this new creation: "See, I will create new heavens and a new earth. The former things will not be remembered, nor will they come to mind. But be glad and rejoice forever in what I will create, for I will create Jerusalem to be a delight and its people a joy. I will rejoice over Jerusalem and take delight in my people; the sound of weeping and of crying will be heard in it no more." This passage underscores the hope of a world restored by God's love.

The Reconciliation of All Things

Colossians 1:19-20 emphasizes the cosmic scope of Christ's redemptive work: "For God was pleased to have all His fullness dwell in Him, and through Him to reconcile to Himself all things, whether things on earth or things in heaven, by making peace through His blood, shed on the cross." This reconciliation signifies the restoration of harmony and love in all of creation.

The Future Hope of Perfect Love

Perfect Love Casts Out Fear

The Absence of Fear and Pain

In God's Kingdom, perfect love will cast out all fear. 1 John 4:18 assures us, "There is no fear in love. But perfect love drives out fear, because fear has to do with punishment. The one who fears is not made perfect in love." The fulfillment of divine love will eliminate fear, pain, and suffering, creating an environment of eternal peace and joy.

Living in the Light of God's Love

Revelation 21:23-24 describes the eternal light of God's love: "The city does not need the sun or the moon to shine on it, for the glory of God gives it light, and the Lamb is its lamp. The nations will walk by its light, and the kings of the earth will bring their splendor into it." In God's Kingdom, His love will be the guiding light for all.

The Communion of Saints

Eternal Fellowship

The Kingdom of God promises eternal fellowship among believers, united in perfect love. Hebrews 12:22-24 paints a picture of this heavenly assembly: "But you have come to Mount Zion, to the city of the living God, the heavenly Jerusalem. You have come to thousands upon thousands of angels in joyful assembly, to the church of the firstborn, whose names are written in heaven. You have come to God, the Judge of all, to the spirits of the righteous made perfect, to Jesus the mediator of a new covenant, and to the sprinkled blood that speaks a better word than the blood of

Abel." This eternal communion reflects the fulfillment of divine love in the community of the redeemed.

Unity with God and Each Other

John 17:20-23 records Jesus' prayer for unity among His followers: "My prayer is not for them alone. I pray also for those who will believe in me through their message, that all of them may be one, Father, just as You are in me and I am in You. May they also be in us so that the world may believe that You have sent me. I have given them the glory that You gave me, that they may be one as we are one—I in them and You in me—so that they may be brought to complete unity. Then the world will know that You sent me and have loved them even as You have loved me." This unity, achieved through divine love, will be fully realized in God's Kingdom.

Implications for Our Lives Today

Living with Hope

Anchoring Our Lives in Future Hope

The future hope of perfect love in God's Kingdom provides a firm anchor for our lives today. Hebrews 6:19 affirms, "We have this hope as an anchor for the soul, firm and secure. It enters the inner sanctuary behind the curtain." This hope encourages us to persevere through trials, knowing that God's perfect love awaits us.

Inspiring Resilience

Romans 8:18 offers perspective: "I consider that our present sufferings are not worth comparing with the glory that will be revealed in us." The promise of future glory and perfect love inspires resilience, helping us endure present difficulties with faith and hope.

Pursuing Holiness and Love

Reflecting God's Love

As we anticipate the fulfillment of love in God's Kingdom, we are called to reflect His love in our lives. 1 John 4:11-12 instructs, "Dear friends, since God so loved us, we also ought to love one another. No one has ever seen God; but if we love one another, God lives in us and His love is made complete in us." Our actions should mirror the divine love we have received.

Growing in Holiness

2 Peter 3:11-12 exhorts, "Since everything will be destroyed in this way, what kind of people ought you to be? You ought to live holy and godly lives as you look forward to the day of God and speed its coming." Living in anticipation of God's Kingdom motivates us to grow in holiness and align our lives with His will.

Engaging in Mission and Service

Advancing God's Kingdom

Our hope in the future fulfillment of love compels us to engage in mission and service. Matthew 28:19-20, the Great Commission, calls us to make disciples of all nations, sharing the love of Christ with the world. By participating in God's redemptive work, we contribute to the advancement of His Kingdom.

Serving Others

Galatians 5:13-14 emphasizes the call to serve: "You, my brothers and sisters, were called to be free. But do not use your freedom to indulge the flesh; rather, serve one another humbly in love. For the entire law is fulfilled in keeping this one command: 'Love your neighbor as yourself.'" Serving others with humility and love reflects the future reality of God's Kingdom in our present lives.

The Transformative Power of Eschatological Love

Personal Transformation

Becoming Christlike

The anticipation of perfect love in God's Kingdom transforms us, making us more like Christ. 1 John 3:2-3 states, "Dear friends, now we are children of God, and what we will be has not yet been made known. But we know that when Christ appears, we shall be like Him, for we shall see Him as He is. All who have this hope in Him purify themselves, just as He is pure." This transformation prepares us for our eternal destiny.

Living with Purpose

Understanding the eschatological fulfillment of love gives our lives purpose. Ephesians 2:10 reminds us, "For we are God's handiwork, created in Christ Jesus to do good works, which God prepared in advance for us to do." Our actions today contribute to the unfolding of God's redemptive plan.

Community Transformation

Building a Kingdom Community

As we live in light of God's future Kingdom, we are called to build communities that reflect His love and justice. Acts 2:42-47 describes the early church as a model: "They devoted themselves to the apostles' teaching and to fellowship, to the breaking of bread and to prayer. Everyone was filled with awe at the many wonders and signs performed by the apostles. All the believers were together and had everything in common. They sold property and possessions to give to anyone who had need. Every day they continued to meet together in the temple courts. They broke bread in their homes and ate together with glad and sincere hearts, praising God and enjoying the favor of all the people. And the Lord added to their number daily those who were being saved."

This vision inspires us to create communities that embody the values of God's Kingdom.

Promoting Justice and Peace

Isaiah 61:1-3 speaks of the Messiah's mission to bring justice and peace: "The Spirit of the Sovereign Lord is on me, because the Lord has anointed me to proclaim good news to the poor. He has sent me to bind up the brokenhearted, to proclaim freedom for the captives and release from darkness for the prisoners, to proclaim the year of the Lord's favor and the day of vengeance of our God, to comfort all who mourn, and provide for those who grieve in Zion—to bestow on them a crown of beauty instead of ashes, the oil of joy instead of mourning, and a garment of praise instead of a spirit of despair. They will be called oaks of righteousness, a planting of the Lord for the display of His splendor." Promoting justice and peace reflects the eschatological hope of God's Kingdom.

The future hope of perfect love in God's Kingdom is a central theme in Christian eschatology, offering profound implications for our lives today. By understanding the biblical foundations of eschatological love, embracing the promise of its fulfillment, and living in anticipation of God's Kingdom, we can experience personal and community transformation.

As we continue to explore the theology of love, let us anchor our lives in the hope of God's future Kingdom, pursue holiness and love, engage in mission and service, and build communities that reflect His justice and peace. Through intentional practices, reliance on God's strength, and a commitment to love, we can embody the love that God calls us to live out, anticipating the day when His perfect love will be fully realized.

## 7.1.0 THE ULTIMATE REALIZATION OF LOVE IN THE NEW HEAVEN AND NEW EARTH

The concept of eschatology, which deals with the end times and the final destiny of humanity, is deeply intertwined with the theology of love. The ultimate realization of love in the New Heaven and New Earth represents the culmination of God's redemptive plan. This chapter explores the biblical vision of the New Heaven and New Earth, the fulfillment of divine love, and the implications for believers as we anticipate this glorious future.

Biblical Vision of the New Heaven and New Earth

The Prophecy of Isaiah

A New Creation

The vision of a new creation is prophesied in the Old Testament. Isaiah 65:17-19 states, "See, I will create new heavens and a new earth. The former things will not be remembered, nor will they come to mind. But be glad and rejoice forever in what I will create, for I will create Jerusalem to be a delight and its people a joy. I will rejoice over Jerusalem and take delight in my people; the sound of weeping and of crying will be heard in it no more." This prophecy speaks of a future where God will create a new reality, free from sorrow and filled with joy.

Peace and Harmony

Isaiah 11:6-9 provides a vision of peace and harmony in this new creation: "The wolf will live with the lamb, the leopard will lie down with the goat, the calf and the lion and the yearling together; and a little child will lead them. The cow will feed with the bear, their young will lie down together, and the lion will eat straw like the ox. The infant will play near the cobra's den, and the young child will put its hand into the viper's nest. They will neither harm nor destroy on all my holy mountain, for the earth will be filled with the knowledge of the Lord as the waters cover the sea." This imagery reflects the ultimate realization of love, where all creation lives in perfect harmony.

Revelation's Vision

The New Jerusalem

The Book of Revelation provides a detailed vision of the New Heaven and New Earth. Revelation 21:1-4 describes this ultimate reality: "Then I saw 'a new heaven and a new earth,' for the first heaven and the first earth had passed away, and there was no longer any sea. I saw the Holy City, the new Jerusalem, coming down out of heaven from God, prepared as a bride beautifully dressed for her husband. And I heard a loud voice from the throne saying, 'Look! God's dwelling place is now among the people, and He will dwell with them. They will be His people, and God Himself will be with them and be their God. He will wipe every tear from their eyes. There will be no more death or mourning or crying or pain, for the old order of things has passed away.'" This passage emphasizes the intimate relationship between God and His people, and the eradication of all suffering.

Eternal Light and Glory

Revelation 21:22-27 continues to describe the New Jerusalem: "I did not see a temple in the city, because the Lord God Almighty and the Lamb are its temple. The city does not need the sun or the moon to shine on it, for the glory of God gives it light, and the Lamb is its lamp. The nations will walk by its light, and the kings of the earth will bring their splendor into it. On no day will its gates ever be shut, for there will be no night there. The glory and honor of the nations will be brought into it. Nothing impure will ever enter it, nor will anyone who does what is shameful or deceitful, but only those whose names are written in the Lamb's book of life." The presence of God and the Lamb as the eternal light signifies the ultimate fulfillment of divine love.

The Fulfillment of Divine Love

God's Dwelling Among His People

Intimate Relationship

The ultimate realization of love is epitomized by God's dwelling among His people. Revelation 21:3 highlights this intimate relationship: "And I heard a loud voice from the throne saying, 'Look! God's dwelling place is now among the people, and He will dwell with them. They will be His people, and God Himself will be with them and be their God.'" This close communion between God and humanity reflects the fulfillment of His love.

Perfect Fellowship

1 Corinthians 13:12 describes the perfect fellowship that believers will experience: "For now we see only a reflection as in a mirror; then we shall see face to face. Now I know in part; then I shall know fully, even as I am fully known." In the New Heaven and New Earth, believers will experience the fullness of God's love and presence, knowing Him fully and being fully known.

The Eradication of Suffering

No More Pain and Sorrow

The eradication of suffering is a key aspect of the fulfillment of divine love. Revelation 21:4 promises, "He will wipe every tear from their eyes. There will be no more death or mourning or crying or pain, for the old order of things has passed away." The removal of all pain and sorrow underscores the complete and perfect love that characterizes God's Kingdom.

Eternal Joy and Peace

Isaiah 35:10 speaks of the eternal joy and peace that will prevail: "And those the Lord has rescued will return. They will enter Zion with singing; everlasting joy will crown their heads. Gladness and joy will overtake them, and sorrow and sighing will flee away." The joy and peace in the New Heaven and New Earth are expressions of the fullness of God's love.

The Restoration of Creation

Harmony and Unity

The New Heaven and New Earth will also see the restoration of all creation. Romans 8:21-22 explains, "That the creation itself will be liberated from its bondage to decay and brought into the freedom and glory of the children of God. We know that the whole creation has been groaning as in the pains of childbirth right up to the present time." The liberation and restoration of creation reflect the pervasive reach of God's redemptive love.

Renewal of All Things

Revelation 21:5 declares, "He who was seated on the throne said, 'I am making everything new!' Then He said, 'Write this down, for these words are trustworthy and true.'" The renewal of all things signifies the ultimate victory of love over decay and death, bringing about a new and perfect order.

Implications for Believers

Living in Anticipation

Hope and Assurance

The promise of the New Heaven and New Earth provides hope and assurance for believers. Hebrews 11:1 defines faith as "confidence in what we hope for and assurance about what we do not see." This future hope encourages believers to live with confidence and anticipation of God's ultimate fulfillment of love.

Motivation for Holiness

2 Peter 3:13-14 exhorts believers to live holy lives in anticipation of this future reality: "But in keeping with His promise we are looking forward to a new heaven and a new earth, where righteousness dwells. So then, dear friends, since you are looking forward to this, make every effort to be found spotless, blameless and at peace with Him." The hope of the

New Heaven and New Earth motivates believers to pursue holiness and righteousness.

Reflecting Divine Love Today

Embodiment of Love

As we anticipate the ultimate realization of love, we are called to reflect divine love in our lives today. 1 John 4:11-12 instructs, "Dear friends, since God so loved us, we also ought to love one another. No one has ever seen God; but if we love one another, God lives in us and His love is made complete in us." By embodying God's love, we provide a glimpse of the future Kingdom.

Acts of Compassion and Justice

Micah 6:8 emphasizes the call to act justly and love mercy: "He has shown you, O mortal, what is good. And what does the Lord require of you? To act justly and to love mercy and to walk humbly with your God." Engaging in acts of compassion and justice reflects the love and values of God's future Kingdom.

Engaging in Mission and Evangelism

Sharing the Good News

The hope of the New Heaven and New Earth compels believers to engage in mission and evangelism. Matthew 28:19-20, the Great Commission, calls us to make disciples of all nations, sharing the love and hope of Christ with the world. By participating in God's redemptive work, we contribute to the realization of His Kingdom.

Building the Kingdom

Through mission and evangelism, believers help build the Kingdom of God on earth. Acts 1:8 promises, "But you will receive power when the Holy Spirit comes on you, and you will be my witnesses in Jerusalem, and in all Judea and Samaria, and to the ends of the earth." As witnesses of Christ's love, we participate in God's plan to bring about the New Heaven and New Earth.

The Transformative Power of Eschatological Love

Personal Transformation

Becoming Like Christ

The anticipation of perfect love in the New Heaven and New Earth transforms us, making us more like Christ. 1 John 3:2-3 states, "Dear friends, now we are children of God, and what we will be has not yet been made known. But we know that when Christ appears, we shall be like Him, for we shall see Him as He is. All who have this hope in Him purify themselves, just as He is pure." This transformation prepares us for our eternal destiny.

Living

with Purpose

Understanding the eschatological fulfillment of love gives our lives purpose. Ephesians 2:10 reminds us, "For we are God's handiwork, created in Christ Jesus to do good works, which God prepared in advance for us to do." Our actions today contribute to the unfolding of God's redemptive plan.

Community Transformation

Building a Kingdom Community

As we live in light of God's future Kingdom, we are called to build communities that reflect His love and justice. Acts 2:42-47 describes the early church as a model: "They devoted themselves to the apostles' teaching and to fellowship, to the breaking of bread and to prayer. Everyone was filled with awe at the many wonders and signs performed by the apostles. All the believers were together and had everything in common. They sold property and possessions to give to anyone who had need. Every day they continued to meet together in the temple courts. They broke bread in their homes and ate together with glad and sincere hearts, praising God and enjoying the favor of all the people. And the Lord added to their number daily those who were being saved." This vision inspires us to create communities that embody the values of God's Kingdom.

Promoting Justice and Peace

Isaiah 61:1-3 speaks of the Messiah's mission to bring justice and peace: "The Spirit of the Sovereign Lord is on me because the Lord has anointed me to proclaim good news to the poor. He has sent me to bind up the brokenhearted, to proclaim freedom for the captives and release from darkness for the prisoners, to proclaim the year of the Lord's favor and the day of vengeance of our God, to comfort all who mourn, and provide for those who grieve in Zion—to bestow on them a crown of beauty instead of ashes, the oil of joy instead of mourning, and a garment of praise instead of a spirit of despair. They will be called oaks of righteousness, a planting of the Lord for the display of His splendor." Promoting justice and peace reflects the eschatological hope of God's Kingdom.

The ultimate realization of love in the New Heaven and New Earth is the culmination of God's redemptive plan, offering a profound vision of future hope and fulfillment. By understanding the biblical vision of this new creation, embracing the fulfillment of divine love, and living in anticipation of this glorious future, believers can experience personal and community transformation.

As we continue to explore the theology of love, let us anchor our lives in the hope of God's future Kingdom, pursue holiness and love, engage in mission and service, and build communities that reflect His justice and peace. Through intentional practices, reliance on God's strength, and a commitment to love, we can embody the love that God calls us to live out, anticipating the day when His perfect love will be fully realized in the New Heaven and New Earth.

## 7.2.0 ETERNAL LOVE AND WORSHIP

The eternal nature of God's love is a central theme in Christian theology and eschatology. It underscores the unending and unwavering character of divine love, which will be fully realized in eternity. This chapter explores the eternal nature of God's love, its expression in eternal worship, and the implications for believers as we anticipate and participate in this everlasting relationship with God.

The Eternal Nature of God's Love

God's Unchanging Love

Everlasting Covenant

God's love is described as everlasting and unchanging in the Bible. Jeremiah 31:3 proclaims, "The Lord appeared to us in the past, saying: 'I have loved you with an everlasting love; I have drawn you with unfailing kindness.'" This covenantal love is unbreakable and eternal, forming the foundation of God's relationship with His people.

Faithfulness Through Generations

Psalm 100:5 affirms the eternal nature of God's love: "For the Lord is good and His love endures forever; His faithfulness continues through all generations." God's love is not limited by time; it extends to all generations, ensuring His faithfulness and commitment to His people throughout eternity.

Manifested Through Christ

The Ultimate Expression of Love

The ultimate expression of God's eternal love is manifested through Jesus Christ. John 3:16 emphasizes this: "For God so loved the world that He gave His one and only Son, that whoever believes in Him shall not perish but have eternal life." The sacrificial love of Christ on the cross is the pinnacle of God's love for humanity, offering eternal life to all who believe.

Perpetual Intercession

Christ's role as our intercessor also demonstrates the eternal nature of God's love. Hebrews 7:24-25 states, "But because Jesus lives forever, He has a permanent priesthood. Therefore He is able to save completely those who come to God through Him, because He always lives to intercede for them." Christ's perpetual intercession ensures that God's love and grace are continually available to us.

Eternal Worship in the Presence of God's Love

Worship in the New Heaven and New Earth

The Heavenly Throne Room

The Book of Revelation provides a vivid depiction of eternal worship in the presence of God's love. Revelation 4:8-11 describes the worship around God's throne: "Each of the four living creatures had six wings and was covered with eyes all around, even under its wings. Day and night they never stop saying: 'Holy, holy, holy is the Lord God Almighty,' who was, and is, and is to come. Whenever the living creatures give glory, honor and thanks to Him who sits on the throne and who lives for ever and ever, the twenty-four elders fall down before Him who sits on the throne and worship Him who lives for ever and ever. They lay their crowns before the throne and say: 'You are worthy, our Lord and God, to receive glory and honor and power, for You created all things, and by Your will they were created and have their being.'" This scene reflects the eternal nature of worship in God's presence.

The Marriage Supper of the Lamb

Revelation 19:6-9 portrays the Marriage Supper of the Lamb, a celebration of the union between Christ and His church: "Then I heard what sounded like a great multitude, like the roar of rushing waters and like loud peals of thunder, shouting: 'Hallelujah! For our Lord God Almighty reigns. Let us rejoice and be glad and give Him glory! For the wedding of the Lamb has come, and His bride has made herself ready. Fine linen, bright and clean, was given her to wear.' (Fine linen stands for the righteous acts of God's holy people.) Then the angel said to me, 'Write this: Blessed are those who are invited to the wedding supper of the Lamb!' And he added, 'These are the true words of God.'" This event symbolizes the eternal celebration of God's love and the ultimate communion between Christ and His followers.

Expressions of Eternal Worship

Unceasing Praise

Eternal worship involves unceasing praise and adoration of God. Psalm 145:1-2 exemplifies this: "I will exalt You, my God, the King; I will praise Your name for ever and ever. Every day I will praise You and extol Your name for ever and ever." The continuous nature of this praise reflects the unending appreciation and reverence for God's eternal love.

Adoration and Thanksgiving

Worship in eternity will also be characterized by adoration and thanksgiving. Ephesians 5:19-20 encourages believers to "speak to one another with psalms, hymns, and songs from the Spirit. Sing and make music from your heart to the Lord, always giving thanks to God the Father for everything, in the name of our Lord Jesus Christ." This attitude of gratitude and worship will be perfected in the presence of God.

Living in the Light of God's Love

The Glory of God as Eternal Light

Revelation 21:23-24 describes the New Jerusalem, where God's glory serves as eternal light: "The city does not need the sun or the moon to shine on it, for the glory of God gives it light, and the Lamb is its lamp. The nations will walk by its light, and the kings of the earth will bring their splendor into it." Living in the light of God's love will be a defining feature of eternity, providing continual illumination and guidance.

Reflecting God's Love

As we anticipate this eternal worship, we are called to reflect God's love in our lives today. 1 John 4:19 states, "We love because He first loved us." Our response to God's eternal love is to love others, mirroring His compassion and grace in our daily interactions.

Implications for Believers

Living with Eternal Perspective

Hope and Assurance

The eternal nature of God's love provides hope and assurance for believers. Romans 8:38-39 assures us, "For I am convinced that neither death nor life, neither angels nor demons, neither the present nor the future, nor any powers, neither height nor depth nor anything else in all creation, will be able to separate us from the love of God that is in Christ Jesus our Lord." This assurance encourages us to live with confidence, knowing that God's love is unchanging and eternal.

Motivation for Worship and Service

Understanding the eternal nature of God's love motivates us to engage in worship and service. Hebrews 12:28-29 encourages, "Therefore, since we are receiving a kingdom that cannot be shaken, let us be thankful, and so worship God acceptably with reverence and awe, for our 'God is a consuming fire.'" Our worship and service are responses to the unending love we have received.

Engaging in Mission and Evangelism

Sharing the Good News

The eternal love of God compels believers to share the good news of Christ with the world. Matthew 28:19-20, the Great Commission, calls us to make disciples of all nations, sharing the love and hope of Christ with everyone. By participating in God's redemptive work, we help others experience His eternal love.

Building the Kingdom

Through mission and evangelism, believers help build the Kingdom of God on earth. Acts 1:8 promises, "But you will receive power when the Holy Spirit comes on you, and you will be my witnesses in Jerusalem, and in all Judea and Samaria, and to the ends of the earth." As witnesses of Christ's love, we contribute to the realization of His eternal Kingdom.

Transforming Personal and Community Life

Personal Transformation

The anticipation of eternal love and worship transforms us, making us more like Christ. 2 Corinthians 3:18 states, "And we all, who with unveiled faces contemplate the Lord's glory, are being transformed into His image with ever-increasing glory, which comes from the Lord, who is the Spirit." This transformation prepares us for our eternal destiny.

Community Transformation

As we live in light of God's eternal love, we are called to build communities that reflect His love and justice. Acts 2:42-47 describes the early church as a model: "They devoted themselves to the apostles' teaching and to fellowship, to the breaking of bread and to prayer. Everyone was filled with awe at the many wonders and signs performed by the apostles. All the believers were together and had everything in common.

They sold property and possessions to give to anyone who had need. Every day they continued to meet together in the temple courts. They broke bread in their homes and ate together with glad and sincere hearts, praising God and enjoying the favor of all the people. And the Lord added to their number daily those who were being saved." This vision inspires us to create communities that embody the values of God's eternal Kingdom.

The eternal nature of God's love is a central theme in Christian eschatology, offering profound implications for our lives today. By understanding the eternal character of divine love, embracing its expression in eternal worship, and living in anticipation of this everlasting relationship with God, believers can experience personal and community transformation.

As we continue to explore the theology of love, let us anchor our lives in the hope of God's eternal love, engage in worship and service, and build communities that reflect His justice and peace. Through intentional practices, reliance on God's strength, and a commitment to love, we can embody the love that God calls us to live out, anticipating the day when His perfect love will be fully realized in the New Heaven and New Earth.

# 7.2.1 WORSHIP AS THE CONSUMMATION OF OUR LOVE FOR GOD

Worship is the ultimate expression and consummation of our love for God. It is both a response to God's immense love and a foretaste of the eternal worship we will experience in the New Heaven and New Earth. This chapter explores the biblical foundations of worship, its role as the consummation of our love for God, and practical implications for believers.

Biblical Foundations of Worship

Worship in the Old Testament

The Tabernacle and Temple

Worship in the Old Testament centered around the Tabernacle and later the Temple. These were places where God's presence dwelled among His people, and where sacrifices and offerings were made as acts of worship. Exodus 25:8-9 explains, "Then have them make a sanctuary for me, and I will dwell among them. Make this tabernacle and all its furnishings exactly like the pattern I will show you." The Tabernacle and Temple were physical representations of God's desire to be with His people and their response in worship.

Psalms of Worship

The Book of Psalms is a rich collection of songs and prayers that express worship to God. Psalm 95:6-7 invites,

"Come, let us bow down in worship, let us kneel before the Lord our Maker; for He is our God and we are the people of His pasture, the flock under His care." The Psalms reflect the heartfelt adoration and reverence for God that characterize true worship.

Worship in the New Testament

Jesus' Teachings on Worship

Jesus redefined worship, emphasizing its spiritual nature. In John 4:23-24, He teaches, "Yet a time is coming and has now come when the true worshipers will worship the Father in the Spirit and in truth, for they are the kind of worshipers the Father seeks. God is spirit, and His worshipers must worship in the Spirit and in truth." Jesus' teachings highlight that worship is not confined to a specific location or ritual but is a heartfelt, spiritual act.

Early Church Worship

The early church practiced communal worship, characterized by teaching, fellowship, breaking of bread, and prayer. Acts 2:42 describes, "They devoted themselves to the apostles' teaching and to fellowship, to the breaking of bread and to prayer." This model of worship reflects the community's dedication to loving and honoring God together.

Worship as the Consummation of Our Love for God

Expressing Our Love for God

Adoration and Praise

Worship is the natural response to God's love, expressing adoration and praise. Psalm 103:1-2 proclaims, "Praise the Lord, my soul; all my inmost being, praise His holy name. Praise the Lord, my soul, and forget not all His benefits." Through worship, we acknowledge God's greatness and express our love and gratitude.

Surrender and Obedience

True worship involves surrender and obedience to God. Romans 12:1 urges, "Therefore, I urge you, brothers and sisters, in view of God's mercy, to offer your bodies as a living sacrifice, holy and pleasing to God—this is your true and proper worship." Offering ourselves as living sacrifices reflects our commitment to living out our love for God through obedience and service.

The Role of Worship in Spiritual Growth

Transformative Power

Worship has a transformative power that shapes our hearts and minds. 2 Corinthians 3:18 states, "And we all, who with unveiled faces contemplate the Lord's glory, are being transformed into His image with ever-increasing glory, which comes from the Lord, who is the Spirit." As we worship, we are changed to become more like Christ, deepening our relationship with God.

Cultivating a Heart of Gratitude

Worship cultivates a heart of gratitude. Colossians 3:16 encourages, "Let the message of Christ dwell among you richly as you teach and admonish one another with all wisdom through psalms, hymns, and songs from the Spirit, singing to God with gratitude in your hearts." Gratitude in worship keeps our focus on God's goodness and faithfulness, fostering a deeper love for Him.

Eternal Worship in the New Heaven and New Earth

The Heavenly Worship Scene

The Book of Revelation provides a glimpse of the eternal worship that will take place in the New Heaven and New Earth. Revelation 7:9-10 describes a great multitude worshiping God: "After this I looked, and there before me was a great multitude that no one could count, from every nation, tribe, people and language, standing before the throne and before the Lamb. They were wearing white robes and were holding palm branches in their hands. And they cried out in a loud voice: 'Salvation belongs to our God, who sits on the throne, and to the Lamb.'" This scene depicts the consummation of our love for God through eternal worship.

Unending Praise and Adoration

Eternal worship will be characterized by unending praise and adoration. Revelation 4:8-11 illustrates this continuous worship: "Each of the four living creatures had six wings and was covered with eyes all around, even under its wings. Day and night they never stop saying: 'Holy, holy, holy is the Lord God Almighty,' who was, and is, and is to come. Whenever the living creatures give glory, honor and thanks to Him who sits on the throne and who lives for ever and ever, the twenty-four elders fall down before Him who sits on the throne and worship Him who lives for ever and ever. They lay their crowns before the throne and say: 'You are worthy, our Lord and God, to receive glory and honor and power, for You created all things, and by Your will they were created and have their being.'" This perpetual worship reflects the eternal nature of our love for God.

Practical Implications for Believers

Living a Life of Worship

Daily Worship

Worship should be a daily practice, not confined to church services. Psalm 34:1 declares, "I will extol the Lord at all times; His praise will always be on my lips." Incorporating worship into our daily routines keeps our hearts aligned with God and continually expresses our love for Him.

Worship through Actions

Our actions can also be acts of worship. Colossians 3:17 instructs, "And whatever you do, whether in word or deed, do it all in the name of the Lord Jesus, giving thanks to God the Father through Him." Serving others, working diligently, and living righteously are all ways to worship God through our daily lives.

Corporate Worship

The Importance of Community Worship

Corporate worship strengthens our faith and fosters a sense of community. Hebrews 10:24-25 emphasizes, "And let us consider how we may spur one another on toward love and good deeds, not giving up meeting together, as some are in the habit of doing, but encouraging one another—and all the more as you see the Day approaching." Gathering with other believers to worship God enhances our spiritual growth and unity.

Diverse Expressions of Worship

Corporate worship can include diverse expressions, such as singing, prayer, reading Scripture, and sacraments. Ephesians 5:19 encourages, "Speak to one another with psalms, hymns, and songs from the Spirit. Sing and make music from your heart to the Lord." Embracing various forms of worship enriches our communal experience and honors God.

### Engaging in Worship with Heart and Mind

#### Intentional Focus

Worship requires intentional focus and engagement. Matthew 22:37 teaches, "Jesus replied: 'Love the Lord your God with all your heart and with all your soul and with all your mind.'" Worshiping with our whole being ensures that our praise is genuine and heartfelt.

#### Meditation and Reflection

Meditating on God's Word and reflecting on His attributes enhance our worship. Psalm 119:15-16 states, "I meditate on your precepts and consider your ways. I delight in your decrees; I will not neglect your word." Deepening our understanding of God through meditation and reflection enriches our worship experience.

### The Transformative Power of Worship

#### Personal Renewal

#### Experiencing God's Presence

Worship brings us into God's presence, where we experience personal renewal. Psalm 16:11 proclaims, "You make known to me the path of life; you will fill me with joy in your presence, with eternal pleasures at your right hand."

Being in God's presence through worship refreshes our spirits and strengthens our faith.

Healing and Restoration

Worship can also bring healing and restoration. Isaiah 61:3 promises, "To provide for those who grieve in Zion—to bestow on them a crown of beauty instead of ashes, the oil of joy instead of mourning, and a garment of praise instead of a spirit of despair." Worshiping God shifts our focus from our troubles to His greatness, bringing comfort and hope.

Community Transformation

Unity and Encouragement

Corporate worship fosters unity and encouragement within the community. Acts 2:42-47 describes the early church's worship and its impact: "They devoted themselves to the apostles' teaching and to fellowship, to the breaking of bread and to prayer. Everyone was filled with awe at the many wonders and signs performed by the apostles. All the believers were together and had everything in common. They sold property and possessions to give to anyone who had need. Every day they continued to meet together in the temple courts. They broke bread in their homes and ate together with glad and sincere hearts, praising God and enjoying the favor of all the people. And the Lord added to their number daily those who were being saved." Worshiping together strengthens bonds and promotes a supportive, loving community.

Inspiring Mission and Service

Worship inspires mission and service. Isaiah 6:8 records Isaiah's response to God's call during a worship experience: "Then I heard the voice of the Lord saying, 'Whom shall I send? And who will go for us?' And I said, 'Here am I. Send me!'" Encountering God in worship motivates us to serve others and share His love.

Worship is the consummation of our love for God, a profound expression of adoration, praise, and surrender. By understanding the biblical foundations of worship, embracing its role as the consummation of our love for God, and living a life of daily and corporate worship, believers can experience personal and community transformation.

As we continue to explore the theology of love, let us commit to worshiping God with our whole being, both individually and collectively. Through intentional practices, heartfelt engagement, and a commitment to love, we can embody the worship that God calls us to live out, anticipating the day when we will worship Him eternally in the New Heaven and New Earth.

CONCLUSION

---

## KEY INSIGHTS ON THE THEOLOGY OF LOVE

Throughout this exploration of the theology of love, we have uncovered the profound and multifaceted nature of divine love as revealed in Scripture. From understanding God's intrinsic nature as love to examining how this love is expressed within the Trinity, we have seen that love is foundational to the very character of God. We have traced the manifestations of divine love in creation, covenant relationships, the life and sacrifice of Jesus Christ, and the workings of the Holy Spirit in the early church.

In the Old Testament, we discovered the steadfast love of God (hesed) in His covenantal relationships with Israel and the prophetic calls to return to that love. In the New Testament, we saw the ultimate expression of divine love through the incarnation, teachings, and sacrificial death of Jesus Christ, emphasizing agape love—selfless and unconditional.

We delved into the transformative power of love in theological reflections, highlighting how love interacts with justice, holiness, and our call to live out divine principles. We examined practical applications of love within family, church, and society, recognizing love as a catalyst for social change and personal transformation.

In eschatological perspectives, we explored the fulfillment of love in the New Heaven and New Earth, where divine love will be perfectly realized, and eternal worship will consummate our love for God. We also reflected on how worship, both now and in eternity, is an ultimate expression of our adoration and gratitude for God's unending love.

Encouraging Readers to Live Out the Theology of Love in Their Daily Lives

The insights gained from this theological journey call us to live out the theology of love in our daily lives. Understanding that God is love and that we are created in His image compels us to reflect His love in our interactions and relationships. Here are practical ways to embody this divine love:

1. Love God with All Your Heart, Soul, and Mind

Make your relationship with God a priority. Spend time in prayer, worship, and studying His Word. As you grow in your love for God, His love will overflow into every aspect of your life.

2. Love Your Neighbor as Yourself

Jesus' command to love our neighbors is foundational. Show kindness, compassion, and empathy to those around you. Seek opportunities to serve and support others, embodying the selfless love of Christ.

3. Forgive and Reconcile

Embrace forgiveness and seek reconciliation in broken relationships. Reflect God's unconditional love by letting go of grudges and extending grace. Strive to restore harmony and unity, both in personal relationships and within the community.

4. Pursue Holiness and Justice

Live a life of integrity, pursuing holiness in thought, word, and deed. Advocate for justice, stand up for the oppressed, and work towards a society that reflects the love and righteousness of God.

5. Engage in Worship

Cultivate a lifestyle of worship, both individually and corporately. Let your worship be an expression of your love and gratitude to God. Engage in heartfelt adoration and live in a way that honors Him daily.

6. Embrace Hope and Anticipation

Live with the hope of the New Heaven and New Earth, where God's love will be fully realized. Let this eschatological hope inspire and motivate you to persevere in faith and love, even in challenging times.

By integrating these principles into our lives, we reflect the divine love that has been so richly poured out on us. As we continue to explore and understand the depth of God's love, let it transform us and guide our actions. In doing so, we become true ambassadors of Christ, sharing His love with the world and bringing glory to God.

May the love of God fill our hearts, guide our steps, and empower us to live out the theology of love every day, until we fully realize His perfect love in eternity.

# APPENDICES

---

## KEY BIBLE VERSES ON LOVE

1. 1 Corinthians 13:4-7 - "Love is patient, love is kind. It does not envy, it does not boast, it is not proud. It does not dishonor others, it is not self-seeking, it is not easily angered, it keeps no record of wrongs. Love does not delight in evil but rejoices with the truth. It always protects, always trusts, always hopes, always perseveres."

2. John 3:16 - "For God so loved the world that He gave His one and only Son, that whoever believes in Him shall not perish but have eternal life."

3. 1 John 4:7-8 - "Dear friends, let us love one another, for love comes from God. Everyone who loves has been born of God and knows God. Whoever does not love does not know God, because God is love."

4. Romans 5:8 - "But God demonstrates His own love for us in this: While we were still sinners, Christ died for us."

5. Matthew 22:37-39 - "Jesus replied: 'Love the Lord your God with all your heart and with all your soul and with all your mind. This is the first and greatest commandment. And the second is like it: Love your neighbor as yourself.'"

6. 1 Peter 4:8 - "Above all, love each other deeply, because love covers over a multitude of sins."

7. Ephesians 5:1-2 - "Follow God's example, therefore, as dearly loved children and walk in the way of love, just as Christ loved us and gave Himself up for us as a fragrant offering and sacrifice to God."

8. Galatians 5:22-23 - "But the fruit of the Spirit is love, joy, peace, forbearance, kindness, goodness, faithfulness, gentleness and self-control. Against such things there is no law."

9. Colossians 3:14 - "And over all these virtues put on love, which binds them all together in perfect unity."

10. Romans 8:38-39 - "For I am convinced that neither death nor life, neither angels nor demons, neither the present nor the future, nor any powers, neither height nor depth nor anything else in all creation, will be able to separate us from the love of God that is in Christ Jesus our Lord."

Recommended Readings on the Theology of Love

1. "The Four Loves" by C.S. Lewis - An exploration of the four types of love described in the Bible: storge

(affection), philia (friendship), eros (romantic love), and agape (divine love).

2. "Love in Hard Places" by D.A. Carson - A thoughtful examination of Christian love in difficult circumstances, including loving one's enemies and dealing with conflict.

3. "The Meaning of Marriage: Facing the Complexities of Commitment with the Wisdom of God" by Timothy Keller - A book that explores the biblical understanding of marriage and love.

4. "Compelled by Love: The Most Excellent Way to Missional Living" by Ed Stetzer and Philip Nation - A guide on how love compels Christians to live missionally and serve others.

5. "The Jesus I Never Knew" by Philip Yancey - Offers a fresh perspective on Jesus' teachings about love, grace, and forgiveness.

6. "Crazy Love: Overwhelmed by a Relentless God" by Francis Chan - A passionate call to experience the full extent of God's love and respond with radical love and obedience.

7. "The Sacred Romance: Drawing Closer to the Heart of God" by Brent Curtis and John Eldredge - Explores the

concept of God's passionate love for humanity and our call to respond to that love.

8. "Life Together: The Classic Exploration of Christian Community" by Dietrich Bonhoeffer - Discusses the role of love in Christian community and fellowship.

9. "The Ragamuffin Gospel: Good News for the Bedraggled, Beat-Up, and Burnt Out" by Brennan Manning - A powerful reminder of God's unconditional love and grace for all people.

10. "Mere Christianity" by C.S. Lewis - Contains profound insights into the nature of Christian love and its implications for our lives.

Discussion Questions for Small Groups and Personal Reflection

1. Understanding God's Love

- How does 1 John 4:7-8 define love, and what does it reveal about God's nature?

- In what ways has God demonstrated His love for humanity? Provide examples from Scripture.

2. Expressions of Love in Our Lives

- How can we practically demonstrate love in our daily interactions with others?

- What challenges do we face in loving others unconditionally, and how can we overcome them?

3. Forgiveness and Reconciliation

- Why is forgiveness essential for reconciliation, and how does it reflect God's love?

- Share a personal experience where you had to forgive someone. How did it impact your relationship with that person?

4. Love in Action

- How can we embody the love described in 1 Corinthians 13 in our personal and community life?

- Discuss practical ways to show love to those in need within your community.

5. Eschatological Hope and Love

- How does the promise of the New Heaven and New Earth influence your understanding of God's love?

- In what ways does the anticipation of eternal worship shape your current worship practices?

6. Living Out the Theology of Love

- Reflect on how you can make worship a daily practice in your life.

- Discuss the importance of corporate worship and how it strengthens your faith and community bonds.

7. Transformative Power of Love

- How has experiencing God's love transformed your life personally?

- In what ways can love be a catalyst for social change and justice in today's world?

8. Love and Holiness

- How do love and holiness intersect in the Christian life?

- What steps can you take to grow in both love and holiness?

9. The Role of the Holy Spirit in Love

- How does the Holy Spirit enable us to love others as Christ loves us?

- Share a time when you felt the Holy Spirit guiding you to act in love.

10. Reflecting on Divine Love

- How can we better understand and appreciate the depth of God's love for us?

- What are some ways we can reflect God's love in our family, workplace, and community?

By engaging with these discussion questions, reflecting on key Bible verses, and exploring recommended readings, we can deepen our understanding and practice of the theology of love. Let us commit to living out this divine love in every aspect of our lives, becoming true ambassadors of Christ's love to the world.

# BIBLIOGRAPHY

1. The Holy Bible, New International Version (NIV). Biblica, Inc. Grand Rapids, MI: Zondervan, 2011.

2. Lewis, C.S. "The Four Loves". New York: Harcourt, Brace, 1960.

3. Carson, D.A. "Love in Hard Places". Wheaton, IL: Crossway, 2002.

4. Keller, Timothy. "The Meaning of Marriage: Facing the Complexities of Commitment with the Wisdom of God". New York: Penguin Books, 2011.

5. Stetzer, Ed and Philip Nation. "Compelled by Love: The Most Excellent Way to Missional Living". Birmingham, AL: New Hope Publishers, 2008.

6. Yancey, Philip. "The Jesus I Never Knew". Grand Rapids, MI: Zondervan, 1995.

7. Chan, Francis. "Crazy Love: Overwhelmed by a Relentless God". Colorado Springs, CO: David C. Cook, 2008.

8. Curtis, Brent, and John Eldredge. "The Sacred Romance: Drawing Closer to the Heart of God". Nashville, TN: Thomas Nelson, 1997.

9. Bonhoeffer, Dietrich. "Life Together: The Classic Exploration of Christian Community". New York: Harper & Row, 1954.

10. Manning, Brennan. "The Ragamuffin Gospel: Good News for the Bedraggled, Beat-Up, and Burnt Out". Sisters, OR: Multnomah Publishers, 1990.

11. Lewis, C.S. "Mere Christianity". New York: HarperOne, 1952.

12. The Holy Bible, English Standard Version (ESV). Wheaton, IL: Crossway, 2001.

13. The Holy Bible, King James Version (KJV). Cambridge Edition: 1769; King James Bible Online, 2021.

14. New Bible Dictionary. 3rd ed. Edited by D.R. W. Wood and I. Howard Marshall. Downers Grove, IL: InterVarsity Press, 1996.

15. Elwell, Walter A., ed. "Evangelical Dictionary of Theology". 2nd ed. Grand Rapids, MI: Baker Academic, 2001.

16. Murray, John. "Redemption Accomplished and Applied". Grand Rapids, MI: Eerdmans, 1955.

17. Piper, John. "Desiring God: Meditations of a Christian Hedonist". Sisters, OR: Multnomah Publishers, 2003.

18. Wright, N.T. "Surprised by Hope: Rethinking Heaven, the Resurrection, and the Mission of the Church". New York: HarperOne, 2008.

19. Packer, J.I. "Knowing God". Downers Grove, IL: InterVarsity Press, 1973.

20. Stott, John. "The Cross of Christ". Downers Grove, IL: InterVarsity Press, 1986.

21. Sproul, R.C. "The Holiness of God". Carol Stream, IL: Tyndale House Publishers, 1985.

22. Eldredge, John. "Wild at Heart: Discovering the Secret of a Man's Soul". Nashville, TN: Thomas Nelson, 2001.

23. Chester, Tim and Steve Timmis. "Total Church: A Radical Reshaping around Gospel and Community". Wheaton, IL: Crossway, 2008.

24. Barclay, William. "The Daily Study Bible Series: The Letters to the Galatians and Ephesians". Philadelphia: Westminster Press, 1976.

25. Guthrie, Donald. "New Testament Theology". Downers Grove, IL: InterVarsity Press, 1981.

26. Geisler, Norman. "Systematic Theology: Volume One, Introduction, Bible". Minneapolis, MN: Bethany House, 2002.

27. Frame, John M. "Systematic Theology: An Introduction to Christian Belief". Phillipsburg, NJ: P&R Publishing, 2013.

28. Fee, Gordon D. "Paul, the Spirit, and the People of God". Peabody, MA: Hendrickson Publishers, 1996.

29. Torrance, Thomas F. "The Christian Doctrine of God: One Being Three Persons". Edinburgh: T&T Clark, 1996.

30. Moloney, Francis J. "Love in the Gospel of John: An Exegetical, Theological, and Literary Study". Grand Rapids, MI: Baker Academic, 2013.

31. Grenz, Stanley J. "The Social God and the Relational Self: A Trinitarian Theology of the Imago Dei". Louisville, KY: Westminster John Knox Press, 2001.

32. Peterson, David. "Engaging with God: A Biblical Theology of Worship". Downers Grove, IL: InterVarsity Press, 1992.

33. Hurtado, Larry W. "At the Origins of Christian Worship: The Context and Character of Earliest Christian Devotion". Grand Rapids, MI: Eerdmans, 1999.

34. Bauckham, Richard. "The Theology of the Book of Revelation". Cambridge: Cambridge University Press, 1993.

35. Moltmann, Jürgen. "The Coming of God: Christian Eschatology". Minneapolis, MN: Fortress Press, 1996.

This comprehensive bibliography provides the sources and references that have informed the exploration of the theology of love in this book. These works offer further depth and insight into the profound nature of divine love and its implications for our lives.

Printed in the USA
CPSIA information can be obtained
at www.ICGtesting.com
CBHW051541111224
18825CB00029B/520

9 798330 595204